All Scripture references taken from the KJV of the Holy Bible, unless otherwise indicated.

PLEAD YOUR CASE: ***A Man's Life Is His Testimony***

by Dr. Marlene Miles

Freshwater Press 2026

Freshwaterpress9@gmail.com

ISBN: 978-1-971933-44-3

Paperback Version

Table of Contents

The court was seated,
and the books were opened.
(Daniel 7:10)

Dedication

To those who have walked through seasons when the truth of their lives was questioned and the record of their faithfulness seemed hidden.

May you remember that nothing lived before God is forgotten and there is nothing hidden from Him.

Every act of integrity is known. Every moment of faithfulness is preserved. Every kindness, every tear is recorded. Every quiet decision to walk in truth becomes part of a testimony that will one day be seen clearly.

Your life is not unnoticed. It is written in the record before God.

INTRODUCTION

Do you swear to tell the truth, the whole truth, and nothing but the truth, so help you, God?

Swearing in.

Testimony.

Some may think this is too morbid of a subject, but it is important.

God will also judge the secrets of the hearts of men--, and women. So, guard your heart with all diligence for out of it come both the issues of life, and also, your heart will tell on you. Men view other men by looking on their faces and external things, but God looks on the heart. Do you think the heart, whether unregenerated and deceitfully wicked or made new in Christ will not answer the One who made it? The heart will tell on you, my friends. Make sure what it says about you is a good report. Be honest with and about yourself now so that when Judgement arrives you will be glad.

The wise thing to do would be to tell on your heart on this side of judgment, so it won't tell on you on the other side. That means repent. Recall, whatever you expose to the light, Light will win. Light wins over darkness every time. So, a secret of the heart is not kept secret in Light, no, it is kept secret in darkness. Repentance brings Light.

His judgment is flawless, righteous, holy, and final. No do-overs after judgment. No one can avoid it. No one can bribe their way out of it. There are no loopholes on that side. So, we get it right on this side. And, Amen.

He sees what no human sees. He knows what no human knows. He is Omniscient; He knows all. This is not Baby Jesus; this is The Christ of God. His judgment is so precise that He divides soul from spirit and thought from intention.

This is not human court. This is divine exposure. And, from what I have heard from people who say they've had near death experience, it is all in an instant. No time to stand and plead your case. The pleading of your case is now, while you are alive and among the living. The pleading of your case are the thoughts of your heart, the things you dwell on or dismiss in your mind. The things you do or don't do that honor or dishonor God and the Word of Truth. This whole life no matter how long it is the time when, Yes, Jesus is your Advocate and you are pleading your case. Right now. Everyday. All day when you can--, 24/7.

IN A MOMENT

People who have reported near-death experiences often describe seeing their entire lives flash before them in an instant. This aligns with the seriousness of Scripture, which teaches that we will give account for every idle word we speak—Jesus Himself said,

> But I tell you that everyone will have to give account on the day of judgment for every empty word they have spoken, (Matthew 12:36).

If every careless word is weighed, how much more the totality of our lives? The question then arises: how can anyone answer for a lifetime in a mere moment?

The premise of this book is that the answers to those future questions are being formed now, in real time, by the way we live. The Bible teaches,

> For God will bring every deed into judgment, including every hidden thing, whether it is good or evil, (Ecclesiastes 12:14).

Our actions, our words, and even our thoughts are all testimonies, speaking on our behalf or against us. The apostle Paul reminds us,

So then, each of us will give an account of ourselves to God, (Romans 14:12).

Plead Your Case is a call to recognize that while we are alive, we are actively testifying—through our choices, our deeds, and our inner thoughts. As Jesus said,

For out of the abundance of the heart the mouth speaks. A good man brings good things out of the good stored up in him, and an evil man brings evil things out of the evil stored up in him, (Matthew 12:34-35).

Our lives are a continual testimony before God. Therefore, now is the time to live honestly and repentantly, allowing the light of Christ to transform us so that when the time comes to give an account, our hearts will bear witness to the Truth and Grace we have embraced.

THE JUDGE

The Christ Who Confronts The Living And The Dead

The world loves the Jesus who heals. They love the Jesus who blesses, the Jesus who feeds, comforts and forgives.

But Scripture also reveals a Jesus many believers ignore, the Judge of all mankind, the Christ before whom every knee will bow, and every life will be measured. He is not just Savior. He is not merely Lamb. He is not merely Teacher, not merely Redeemer, but the Christ that fills all in all—the everything Christ.

Christ wasn't simple; He was loving, wise, discerning, bold, and boundary-strong. Christ wasn't simple; He was strategic. Christ wasn't simple; He was love with a spine.

Modern culture often wants a flat, one-dimensional, "nice guy" Jesus, but the Biblical Jesus was compassionate yet confrontational. He was gentle yet fierce. He was forgiving yet truthful, humble yet authoritative, approachable yet unmanipulable, sacrificial yet deeply boundaried. Jesus is not a simple study; He is multi-layered, multi-faceted. He is patient yet unwavering, peaceful yet unwilling to tolerate sin. He is not a baby.

People want Christians to reflect a watered-down Jesus… they think Christianity means NICE. But the real Christ was complex, multidimensional, and strong.

This is why people oversimplify him. it could be that they haven't studied much more about Jesus since Sunday School when they were 10. Most people aren't rejecting the real Christ—they're rejecting the simplified, sanitized, children's-picture-book version they were taught when they were ten.

People oversimplify Christ because they were first taught a child's version of Him. Far too many adults are still relating to a Jesus they met in Sunday School—a Jesus who was reduced to gentle stories, flannelgraph murals and morals, "be nice" lessons, safe parables, and simplified theology designed for children. That Jesus was appropriate if your age is 10, but not for age 30, 50, or 80.

The real Jesus—the One in Scripture—is far too complex, too fierce, too intentional, too multidimensional to fit inside the children's version. Jesus is not SIMPLE. You can't simplify Him to a manger and leave Him there. Jesus is not SIMPLE – He is Merciful to come down to our level so we can begin to understand – That is why we were introduced to Him as we were when we were kids. But our understanding and knowledge of Him should be evolving and increasing every day.

People may oversimplify Him if their understanding hasn't grown since they first met Him. They learned "Jesus loves me" (but never learned *how* He loves, *why* He loves, or *what* His Love requires).

God is Love. Jesus is Love. But Love is not just a feeling, it is a power; it is the greatest power in the entire universe.

> Three things will last forever—faith, hope, and love—and the greatest of these is love. (1 Corinthians 13:13 NLT)

They learned He's gentle (but we also know that He is also a consuming fire). He is the Judge of the living and the dead. He confronts every soul with an inescapable truth: There is nothing hidden that will not be revealed.

Judgment is not a threat, it is the final expression of His Holiness. Jesus said, **"The Father judges no one, but has committed all judgment to the Son."** All judgment.

The Throne will not display the Father's wrath and the Son's Mercy. The same Christ who carried the Cross will carry the gavel. This is the fullness of His office as the Christ of God:

- **Lamb** — to save
- **Lion** — to rule
- **Judge** — to conclude

Holiness demands judgment. Love demands justice. Truth demands accountability. Jesus is all three.

The living and the dead stand before one **Man.** Scripture says that we must all appear before the judgment seat of Christ. There is more than one judgment. First the wheat will be separated from the tares, then those who are in Christ will be judged for their works – or lack of works.

Who must appear? Everyone. the righteous and the wicked. Kings and beggars will appear. Prophets, apostles, atheists, agnostics will all be judged. Angels, nations, rulers, all will be judged. Friends, enemies, families, unbelievers and believers – everyone. Because of judgment, that should be a compelling reason for all to get saved. Maybe you shouldn't think like this, but if you think your enemy will be going to Hell, then you should get saved and let the Lord transform your life now so you won't have to be there with them---,***for all eternity. Make your election sure.***

He will judge **the living and the dead** because His authority spans every realm. Every realm of Heaven and Earth, and Hell. Both what is seen and unseen. All things will be judged. No one escapes His jurisdiction because He is Lord of all realms.

He judges according to Truth. Not by appearance – pretty privilege doesn't apply to God. In the Old Testament, wasn't Absalom about the finest man ever? It didn't end very well for him, though, did it? Emotions and tears at that time won't move God. Wealth? Can't buy your way in to Heaven or your way out of hell if you don't like the destination that you've chosen by your own actions and lifestyle.

When Christ judges, motives matter. Secrets matter; they will be exposed. Integrity matters. Hidden obedience matters. unseen faithfulness matters. private sins matter—even iniquity that you carry that is hidden to you. Did you seek the Lord to find out if there was iniquity in your bloodline? Did you care anything about your bloodline, or just yourself? Private righteousness matters

He sees what no human sees. He knows what no human knows. He is Omniscient; He knows all. This is not Baby Jesus; this is The Christ of God. His judgment is so precise that He divides soul from spirit and thought from intention.

This is not human court. This is divine exposure. And, from what I have heard from people who say they've had near death experience, it is all in an instant. No time to stand and plead your case. The pleading of your case is now, while you are alive and among the living. The pleading of your case are the thoughts of your heart, the things you dwell on or dismiss in your mind. The things you do or don't do that honor or dishonor God and the Word of Truth. This whole life no matter how long it is, is the time when you should be "pleading your case." Yes, Jesus is your Advocate, and you are pleading your case. Right now. Everyday. All day when you can--, 24/7.

Believers are judged for reward, not Condemnation. The judgment seat of Christ (the *Bema*) is not about salvation. Believers are judged for faithfulness, obedience, stewardship, calling, motives. Did they submit fully to the Lord? They are judged for purity, and endurance: did they finish well? Believers will also be judged on love (*agape*) and sacrifice.

He will test each life: "Every man's work will be revealed by Fire." Some will shine like gold. Some will burn like straw. But the Fire doesn't condemn, it reveals. Even those whose works burn will still be saved. If you believed, you will be saved. But your works are judged whether they be hay, wood, or stubble for reward, that is eternal crowns.

The wicked are judged for condemnation, because they rejected life.

The Great White Throne judgment is where Christ confronts those who rejected Him. Books are opened; records are read. Deeds are weighed. Every secret is exposed. Every rebellion answered. The Word says we will have to give account for every idle word spoken.

There is no defense because every mouth will be stopped. Christ judges not with cruelty, but with perfect justice. He does not cast souls out of Heaven. He ratifies the eternal direction they chose on Earth. Judgment is the final confirmation of human will.

He will judge angels as well. Paul says, "Do you not know that we shall judge angels?"

Not we alone, we judge under the authority and leadership of Christ Himself. Fallen angels, rebellious *spirits*, and demonic powers stand not only under His condemnation, but under the testimony of the redeemed. The Christ of God confronts every realm of rebellion—human and angelic.

The Judge wears the scars. Judgment and Mercy meet in One Person. The Judge before whom all must stand still bears the wounds that purchased salvation. This is His Glory. The scars remind Heaven of Mercy. The Throne reminds Heaven of authority. The Cross reminds Heaven of Love. The gavel reminds Heaven of justice. He judges with hands that were pierced for the world.

No one will ever be able to say, "You didn't love me." "You didn't pursue me." "You didn't warn me." "You didn't give me a chance." The scars silence every accusation.

His judgment restores the universe. Judgment is not about destruction. It is about **restoration**. Christ judges to purge evil, establish righteousness, restore creation, heal the cosmos, overthrow darkness, vindicate the faithful, fulfill prophecy, prepare the new Heaven and New Earth.

Judgment is God's final act of Love toward a universe He refuses to abandon.

Judgment confronts the living with urgency, and the dead with Truth. For the living, time remains.

repentance is possible. Mercy is available, destiny can shift; life can change.

For the dead, the record stands, the decision is sealed, eternity is set. Christ confronts both with the reality of His Throne.

He confronts the living with Mercy,
and confronts the dead with Truth.

THE OFFICE

In a dream I arrived at a building that resembled a dental office where I had once practiced. I was in a car, initially seated in the back while someone else drove and a tall quiet slim man was in the front passenger's seat. When we pulled into the parking lot, I noticed a long black silt fence bordering the property—the kind used at construction sites to contain soil while land is being disturbed. We parallel parked by it. I evaluated the driver's parking, standing behind the vehicle with the slim quiet man.

When we entered the building, that slim man walked quietly beside me. He said almost nothing, but once inside, he listened and observed as we moved through the rooms.

At one point I explained to him that the office records had once been compromised—our server had been stolen and accessed improperly. I showed him the area where the network equipment was mounted. Lights blinked from several devices attached to the wall. Nearby, the office manager sat taking notes as I spoke. It felt as though testimony was being quietly placed on record.

As we moved through the office, I noticed something strange. The walls in the current space were smooth and pale blue, but one woman was attempting to climb a rough orange stucco wall—the same texture that had existed in and old office of mine years earlier. She could not climb it. She fell and then said her leg was not working properly.

I went to what had once been my office and gathered my things: a coat, another jacket, my purse, and a gray sweatshirt. I placed them all over my left arm and prepared to leave. I walked to the elevator, noticing several birds wandering through the corridor—pigeons and other strange-looking birds moving about on the floor. I simply walked around them and continued toward the elevator.

That is not every detail of that dream, but it is enough.

What struck me later was the order of what had taken place. The environment had been revisited. Testimony had been given. A witness had observed. Evidence had been shown. The record had been written.

No argument was required. No confrontation was necessary. The matter had simply been placed on record. And once the testimony of a matter has been established, a person is free to move forward.

In the Court of God, a man does not stand only on his words; he stands on the testimony of his life.

What really happened in that dream was the invitation to state my case. *What case?*

I had diligently sought the Lord regarding a matter or matters concerning this particular office.

Scripture contains a remarkable invitation from God:

> Put Me in remembrance; let us contend together;
> **state your case**, that you may be acquitted.
> (Isaiah 43:26)

The Lord is not inviting clever argument or persuasive speech. He is inviting truth to be presented before Him. In the Courts of Heaven, a matter is not established by rumor, emotion, or the loudest voice. It is established by testimony and witness.

A life lived in integrity becomes evidence. Faithfulness leaves a record. What has truly happened does not disappear simply because others misunderstand it, distort it, or attempt to hide it.

That is why Scripture repeatedly speaks of books being opened, witnesses standing, and records being examined. God's justice does not depend on human memory or opinion. It rests on what is known and remembered before Him.

When a matter has been truthfully presented and witnessed, the believer does not need to remain trapped in endless defense. The record stands. When the record stands, a person is free to move forward.

In the court of God, the most powerful testimony a person carries is not a speech. It is the life he has lived.

A man's life is his testimony.

My point is that we are giving account every day 24/7--, even in our dreamscapes, and in every choice we make. (Hence, the witnesses, dreams, life's incidences, etc. are answering questions all the time.)

We are not only giving account at the end of life. **Our lives are answering the questions every day.**

My dream illustrated the same three pillars that appear in Scripture whenever truth is examined:

1. **Witness**
2. **Record**
3. **Testimony**

I presented the facts.

The witness observed.

The record existed.

And then I left the scene of the testimony or the record. That is almost the exact structure of a case being placed before a court.

We will talk about this at length in this book.

THE ACCOUNT IS NOT GIVEN ONLY AT THE END

Many people who have had near-death experiences describe a moment when their entire life appears before them. Some say every word, every action, and every decision becomes visible all at once.

A man once told me that when he saw the events of his life laid out before him, he realized something sobering. "There is no way to answer all that," he said. In a sense, he was right. That is, if he had to speak. Doesn't the Word say to let one's works speak for them? If a person had to suddenly explain every decision, every motive, and every action at the end of life, the weight of that moment would be overwhelming.

Scripture suggests something different. The account is not given only at the end. It is being given **every day**. The wise say, Begin with the end in mind. This is a good time to heed that counsel. Our own lives are living proof, living accounts for questions that will ultimately arise. If we are teachable, we let the Word of God, the Holy Spirit and even others help us know and see those questions, so we make right choices throughout life.

Jesus said:

For every idle word men may speak, they will give account of it in the day of judgment.
(Matthew 12:36)

That statement can sound frightening if we imagine the account happening only in a single moment at the end of life.

But the Bible also shows that a person's life is constantly bearing witness. Our choices speak. Our conduct speaks. Our responses to difficulty speak. Day by day, the testimony of a life is forming. In that sense, the account is not something we suddenly invent at the end of our lives. It is something we have been living all along.

Witnesses are with us everyday--, a great cloud of witnesses. The Scriptures describe many kinds of witnesses. There are people who observe, written records, the memory of events, and even Heaven itself. Earth keeps a record, and Jesus once said that even the stones could cry out as witnesses if necessary. Life itself becomes filled with moments that quietly record what is true. A conversation. A decision made when we may think that no one was watching. A choice between integrity and convenience--, each one answers a question.

The record of a life. That is why the Bible repeatedly speaks of books. Daniel saw the Court of Heaven seated and the books opened. Revelation describes a day when people are judged according to what was written in the books.

Those images remind us that the story of a life is not lost. It is recorded. But that record is not merely a list of accusations. It is the testimony of a life. A man's faithfulness. A man's character. A man's choices.

We are living the answer. When we understand this, something changes. We stop thinking of the final judgment as a moment when we must suddenly invent a defense. Instead, we realize something much simpler and more profound: **We are living our testimony now.**

As the Lamb was slain before the foundation of the world, and then years later Jesus came in the volume of the Book where it was written of Him; so do we. It seems God began with the end in mind; He is Alpha and Omega.

Every act of integrity answers a question. Every decision to walk uprightly becomes part of the record. And when the time comes to stand before God, the believer does not need to produce a speech. The testimony of a life will already be there.

Life itself is the testimony. You will not have to invent your defense before God, because your life has already been giving its testimony.

GIVE ACCOUNT

Now if any man build upon this foundation gold, silver, precious stones, wood, hay, stubble; Every man's work shall be made manifest: for the day shall declare it, because it shall be revealed by fire; and the fire shall try every man's work of what sort it is. (1 Corinthians 3:12-13)

We are to give account, does that mean that we will be *talking*? Many accounts are written down, often on a Balance Sheet. Or will the works speak for us? Or is it a combo? The man who wants to or has to 'explain' what will he be saying? The truth? Or what he *thinks*? Or what he wishes? Or what he thinks he can get away with?

Works are examined first.

Every man's work shall be made manifest: for the day shall declare it… and the fire shall try every man's work of what sort it is. (1 Corinthians 3:13)

The focus is not on a person defending themselves verbally. The focus is on the work itself being revealed and tested. The language is almost like evidence placed in the open: the work is made manifest, the day declares it, the fire tests it. The work speaks.

Scripture Also Says We Give Account. At the same time, the Bible does say that people will give account.

Every one of us shall give account of himself to God. (Romans 14:12)

Jesus said:

Every idle word that men shall speak, they shall give account thereof in the day of judgment. (Matthew 12:36)

So, the idea of accountability is clearly present. Notice this: Giving account does not necessarily mean making a persuasive verbal defense. It means being answerable. **The record exists already.** The record of a life already exists. Other passages suggest that a person's life has already been recorded.

The books were opened… and the dead were judged according to their works by the things which were written in the books. (Revelation 20:12)

Here again the emphasis is not on explanations, but on what is written. The testimony is already present. At this point, explanations would be weak. If someone tried to explain their life in that moment, what would they even say? Would they tell the truth? Would they present the motives they wished they had? Would they attempt to reinterpret their actions? Or would they say what they thought might help them escape judgment? Far too often, human explanations are not reliable evidence. That is why Scripture repeatedly emphasizes **works** rather than arguments. The works are the proof.

The life itself speaks.

By their fruits you will know them. (Matthew 7:16)

Fruit is visible evidence. A tree does not need to explain itself because its fruit reveals what it is.

The likely combination may be reached by putting these passages together. The record of the life already exists. The works are revealed and tested. The person is present and answerable before God. But the decisive factor is not how well someone explains themselves; it is what their life actually produced.

If a man had to suddenly construct a defense for his entire life, it would be impossible. But (or therefore) the testimony is not constructed at the end. It is written through the life itself. A man's life is his testimony.

Paul does not say that every man will stand and explain what he built. He says that the work itself will be made manifest. The day will declare it, and the fire will reveal what sort it is. Fire does not ask for explanation. Fire simply tests substance. Gold remains. Silver endures. Precious stones survive the flame. Wood, hay, and stubble disappear without argument. In that moment, the question will not be how a man explains his life, but what his life actually produced. The work will speak for itself.

In the end, a man will not be judged by the explanation he gives, but by the life he lived. When the day comes, the testimony will not be spoken for the first time. It will already have been written in the works of a life. When the fire reveals the work, the testimony will already be in evidence.

When the fire reveals the work, the testimony will already be in evidence. At that moment, a man will not plead his case with words. His life will plead it for him.

When the fire reveals the work, the testimony will already be in evidence.

At that moment, a man will not plead his case with words. His life will plead it for him. A man's life is his testimony.

Lord, let my life speak for me. Let my life speak well for me and of me, in the Name of Jesus.

May my living not be in vain, for I worked while it was day. For the time comes when night falls and no man can work. In that hour, the works themselves will remain—those things built of gold, silver, and precious stones. The labor of a life lived in truth will stand as its testimony.

I must work the works of Him that sent me, while it is day: the night cometh, when no man can work.
(John 9:4)

Let my life speak for me, for when the day of testing comes, the works that remain will plead the case.

THE THRONE AND THE COURT

When people think about God, they often imagine Him as Father, Shepherd, or King. All of those images do appear throughout Scripture. The Bible uses another image just as often—one that many people overlook. God is also revealed as Judge. Again and again the Scriptures describe His throne not only as a seat of authority but as a seat of justice.

The Lord shall endure forever;
He has prepared His throne for judgment.
He shall judge the world in righteousness,
and He shall administer judgment for the peoples in uprightness. (Psalm 9)

The Throne of God is not merely symbolic power. It is the place where truth is examined and justice is rendered. One of the clearest pictures of a courtroom in Heaven appears in the Book of Daniel. The prophet saw a vision that reads like the opening of a courtroom.

I watched till thrones were put in place,
and the Ancient of Days was seated…
the court was seated, and the books were opened.
(Daniel 7:9–10)

The scene contains all the elements of a court. The Judge seated on the Throne. Witnesses standing. Records opened, and matters were examined. This vision reveals something profound about the nature of God's Justice.

Heaven does not operate by rumor; it operates by record; there are **books that remember.** Scripture repeatedly refers to books kept before God. Malachi speaks of a Book of Remembrance written before Him for those who fear the Lord. Daniel saw books opened before judgment. Revelation describes a day when people are judged according to what was written in the books.

These passages remind us that nothing about a life is ultimately forgotten. Every act of faithfulness is remembered. Every injustice is known. Every truth is preserved. We keep books like that here on Earth, as well. Some are good and sentimental, others may be records of the Earthly courts that may not be so flattering to those listed in them.

The Accuser and the Advocate. The courtroom imagery of Scripture **also** includes another figure: the accuser. The name "Satan" literally means, *accuser*. In the book of Job, we see him bringing accusations before God, but the New Testament reveals another figure standing in that same Court.

If anyone sins, we have an **Advocate with the Father**,
Jesus Christ the righteous.
(1 John 2:1)

An advocate is someone who speaks on behalf of another. Christ does not merely save; He also defends. A

Court governed by Truth. Understanding this courtroom language changes the way we see justice. Human courts can lose evidence. Human courts can be influenced by rumor, emotion, or power. The Court of God is governed by something much deeper: Truth. And truth is established through **testimony**. This is why Scripture repeatedly points back to the record of a person's life. Ultimately the testimony of a life is what will be looked at. Ecclesiastes says that God will bring every work into judgment.

Jesus said that people will give account even for the words they speak. Those statements do not exist to frighten us. They exist to remind us of something profound: Life itself becomes evidence. The record of a man's choices, character, and faithfulness becomes the testimony that stands before God.

Which means something very important for every Believer. When the time comes to stand before the Judge, a person will not need to invent a defense. The testimony of their life will already be present.

The beginning of a case brings us back to the invitation God gives in Isaiah: **"State your case."** God is not asking for clever arguments. He is asking for truth to be presented. The question is not simply what a person will say.

The deeper question is: *What does the record show?* In the Court of God, a man's life is his testimony.

THE ACCUSER

If there is a court, there will also be accusations. Scripture does not pretend otherwise. From the earliest pages of the Bible to the final book of Revelation, the people of God encounter accusation—sometimes openly, sometimes subtly, sometimes through human voices, and sometimes through spiritual opposition.

Understanding accusation is essential to understanding how a case is brought before God, because a case rarely begins with testimony. It usually begins with a charge.

The Bible reveals something striking about the enemy of God's people. Satan's role of accuser appears clearly in the Book of Job.

> Now there was a day when the sons of God came to present themselves before the Lord, and Satan also came among them. (Job 1:6)

In that scene, Satan arrives as a prosecutor. He questions Job's integrity. He challenges Job's motives. He suggests that Job's faithfulness is not genuine. The accusation is simple: Job only serves God because his life is comfortable. It is a legal argument against the character of a man. Accusation is strategic and often follows a predictable pattern. First, a question is raised about a person's motives. Then suspicion spreads. Finally, a narrative forms that presents the accusation as truth. This pattern appears throughout Scripture. Joseph was accused in Egypt. David was accused by Saul. Jeremiah was accused by those who rejected his message. Even Jesus Himself faced accusations brought by those who sought to discredit Him. Accusation is one of the oldest strategies used against truth.

Sometimes accusation involves more than words. Sometimes it involves distorting the record itself. Facts are rearranged. Events are reinterpreted. Important details disappear. What actually happened becomes difficult for others to see. But the Scriptures remind us that truth is not determined by the loudest voice.

Truth is determined by what is known before God. This is why the Bible repeatedly speaks of books being opened and records being examined. The final judgment does not depend on the narrative created by human opinion. It depends on what is written in the record.

Anyone who has experienced accusation knows how exhausting defending yourself can be, especially if you are trying to defend yourself against something that didn't even happen. There is a constant temptation to defend oneself against every claim, every rumor, every misunderstanding, but the Bible presents a different perspective. The Believer does not need to answer every accusation in the court of men, because there is another court. A higher Court. In that Court, the case does not rest on argument alone. It rests on testimony. Over time, the record of a life begins to speak louder than the accusations surrounding it. Faithfulness becomes visible. Character becomes evident. The truth that once seemed buried begins to surface. In the end, accusation cannot erase what a life has consistently demonstrated. The testimony remains.

The Court that matters most. This does not mean accusations never hurt. They can wound reputations. They can disrupt relationships. They can create seasons of confusion and hardship. But the Believer's confidence does not rest in winning every argument on Earth. It rests in knowing that the final judgment belongs to God, who judges according to Truth.

So, do you want to be right or righteous?

When a person understands this, something changes. It is the beginning of vindication; the constant need to argue begins to fade. The anxiety of defending every detail begins to loosen its grip. Instead, a quiet confidence grows. The record of a life lived before God will stand. In the end, accusation may begin a case, but testimony finishes it.

There are many different kinds of courts. The highest, of course, is the Court of Heaven, God's Court, a divine tribunal where God judges with perfect knowledge, righteousness and justice.

There is the court of man which most often describes public, Earthly courts like the kind they make many TV shows and movies about. We believe most of them are just, but not all of them are.

Scripture also recognizes human courts, which exist to administer justice among people. Examples include the judges appointed in Israel (Deuteronomy 16:18). There were Roman tribunals before which Jesus and Paul appeared (recorded in the Gospel of John and Acts of the Apostles). These courts can be just or unjust because they depend on human judgment.

There are also hidden, occultic and evil "courts." They may conduct unjust or Corrupt Proceedings. Terms such as "kangaroo court" or "mock court" are modern ways of describing proceedings that *look like a trial but lack fairness*. They aren't separate types of courts in a formal sense; they describe abuse of justice. Your life is not speaking for you to evil doers; most often it is what you are on 'trial' for--- for your Faith and beliefs, your gender, the color of your skin, or some trumped up charge. Only the Mercy of God can save a man from this kind of evil. Pray.

The Bible itself shows examples of unjust trials—for instance, the religious hearing that led to Jesus' crucifixion—but it doesn't classify them as a separate category of court. They are simply human courts acting unjustly. There is also the court of public opinion which we will talk about later in this book.

There are courts that many know nothing about; they are unseen. They could be found in covens on in occultic places where a person could be on "trial" and a witchcraft judgment (for example) could be issued and the person doesn't know that anything even happened, until untoward things start to happen in that person's life. Witches, for example, look for iniquity in (or on) a man to decide if they can move forward in making him their victim. Only God can save a man from this kind of unseen evil. Repent to God and pray.

THE ADVOCATE

If there is an accuser in the court, there must also be a defender. Scripture does not leave the Believer standing alone before accusation. The Bible reveals that in the very court where charges may be raised, there is also One who speaks on behalf of those who belong to God.

> If anyone sins, we have an Advocate with the Father,
> Jesus Christ the righteous.
> (1 John 2:1)

The word *advocate* is legal language. It refers to someone who speaks in defense of another, someone who represents a person's case before the judge. In earthly courts, an advocate may present arguments, introduce evidence, and appeal to the law. In the Court of God, Christ Himself fulfills this role.

This is one of the most profound assurances given to the Believer. The same Court where accusation may arise is also the place where Christ stands as Defender. The Believer does not face the proceedings alone. The One who knows the truth perfectly also speaks on behalf of those who trust Him.

Understanding this changes the way we think about judgment. Many people imagine standing before God as a moment of terror, as if they must suddenly invent a defense for every mistake and failure of their lives. The Gospel reveals something very different. The Believer's defense is not a speech prepared at the last moment. It is the work of Christ combined with the testimony of a life lived in response to that Grace.

The Advocate does not deny the existence of weakness or failure. Scripture is honest about the reality of human imperfection. Instead, Christ stands as the one who has satisfied the demands of Justice and who intercedes for those who belong to Him. The Cross itself becomes the foundation of that defense.

Because of this, the Believer does not approach the court of God with arrogance or despair. He approaches it with confidence grounded in Truth. Christ's advocacy does not erase the importance of a life lived faithfully, but it ensures that the Believer's standing before God does not depend on perfection. It depends on Redemption; it depends on the Blood of Jesus.

This also reveals something important about accusation. The accuser attempts to define a person entirely by failure. The Advocate, however, presents the whole truth. He speaks not only of what has gone wrong but also of what has been redeemed, restored, and transformed.

The Court of God therefore operates differently from the courts of men. Human systems may focus only on what can be proven in the moment. God sees the entire story of a life. He sees the motives of the heart, the moments of repentance, the quiet acts of faithfulness that no one else noticed.

In that light, the Believer's life becomes a testimony not only of human effort but of Divine Grace at work. The Advocate does not simply argue on behalf of a client. He reveals the deeper truth of what God has done in a person's life.

This understanding frees the believer from the exhausting attempt to justify himself before every accusation that arises on Earth. While it is wise to live with integrity and to correct misunderstandings when possible, the final defense of a believer does not rest in public opinion. It rests in the advocacy of Christ and the record of a life lived before God.

Over time, the testimony of that life becomes visible. Faithfulness begins to answer accusations without the need for constant argument. Character becomes evidence. The truth, which may have been questioned for a season, gradually becomes clear.

In this way, the work of the advocate and the testimony of a life begin to converge. Christ intercedes, and the life of the Believer increasingly reflects the reality of that Grace.

This is why the Scriptures encourage believers not merely to defend themselves with words but to live in a way that demonstrates truth. The testimony of a life is not created in a single moment of explanation. It is built day by day, decision by decision, through a pattern of faithfulness.

When the accuser speaks, the Advocate answers. When the record is examined, the story of redemption is present within it. When the final judgment is rendered, it is rendered by a Judge who sees the full truth and who has provided the defense Himself.

For the Believer, this means that the courtroom of God is not merely a place of scrutiny. It is also a place of Mercy that does not weaken justice. It fulfills it.

THE WITNESSES

Every court depends on witnesses. Without witnesses, accusations remain only claims. Testimony cannot be confirmed, and truth becomes difficult to establish. This is why the Scriptures consistently emphasize the role of witnesses whenever a matter is examined.

The principle appears early in the law given to Israel. In Deuteronomy we read:

A matter must be established by the testimony of two or three witnesses. (Deuteronomy 19:15)

This standard protected justice. A single voice could not determine the outcome of a case. Truth required confirmation. It required observation. It required testimony that could stand when examined.

This principle did not disappear with the Old Testament law. Jesus Himself referred to it when speaking about disputes among believers, and Apostle Paul relied on the same principle when addressing matters in the early church. The idea remained the same: truth becomes clear when it is confirmed by witnesses.

But when we examine Scripture closely, we discover that witnesses are not limited to people standing in a courtroom. The Bible describes many kinds of witnesses.

Sometimes the witness is a person who saw what happened. At other times the witness is a written record. In some cases, even the events of a person's life become a form of testimony that confirms what is true. In this way the idea of witnesses expands beyond the courtroom and into everyday life.

A decision made in private becomes a witness to character. A pattern of faithfulness over time becomes a witness to integrity. Even the way a person responds under pressure reveals something that cannot easily be hidden.

Life begins to speak. This is why the Scriptures often describe the world itself as *bearing witness*. In one place, Heaven and Earth are called to stand as witnesses to the covenant between God and His people. In another passage, Jesus declares that if His followers were silent, the stones themselves would cry out.

These statements remind us that truth has a way of revealing itself. A life lived in the open cannot remain hidden forever. The pattern of that life eventually becomes visible to those who observe it.

Sometimes this process takes time. In moments of conflict or accusation, it may appear as though the loudest voice will win. Rumors spread quickly. Narratives form before all the facts are known. In those moments it can feel as if truth has been buried beneath confusion.

But the principle of witnesses reminds us that truth is not determined by the speed of a rumor. It is established by what can stand when examined.

Witnesses emerge over time.

People who have watched closely begin to recognize what is genuine. The record of events becomes clearer. What was once uncertain begins to resolve into something solid and trustworthy. For this reason, Scripture often encourages patience when dealing with accusation or misunderstanding. A life lived faithfully will eventually produce witnesses. Those witnesses may appear in unexpected ways.

Sometimes they appear through the testimony of others who have seen a person's character over many years. Sometimes they appear through written records that preserve what actually happened. Sometimes they appear through the simple consistency of a life that refuses to abandon integrity.

The important truth is this: a person does not need to manufacture witnesses. They arise naturally from the record of a life. This is why a life of integrity carries such quiet power. It creates testimony that cannot easily be erased. Even when accusations arise, the witnesses formed by years of faithful living begin to answer those accusations.

Over time, the truth becomes visible.

The believer who understands this principle no longer feels compelled to control every narrative or correct every misunderstanding immediately. While it is wise to speak truth when necessary, the ultimate confirmation of that truth does not depend solely on a moment of explanation.

It depends on the witnesses that a life produces.

In the court of God, those witnesses matter. They form part of the record that will eventually be examined. They confirm what is genuine and expose what is false. They demonstrate the difference between a momentary accusation and a life that has consistently walked in truth.

When those witnesses stand together, the testimony of a life becomes unmistakable. A matter is established.

THE FALSE WITNESS

This happens often in both human courts and human relationships: people try to control the narrative before the evidence appears. In other words, they pre-testify. They tell a story first, hoping that when the facts eventually surface, people will interpret those facts through the story they already planted.

This is an old human strategy. People who are trying to control the outcome of a situation often do three things: They speak first. Whoever speaks first often frames the story. Narrative Before Evidence. They define the interpretation. They tell people what the events "mean." They pre-position themselves as the victim or hero.

So, when the real evidence emerges, listeners are already thinking: "Ah, this must be what they were talking about." But that kind of testimony is made only of words.

Scripture warns about this. The Bible recognizes this phenomenon very clearly. Proverbs makes an almost courtroom observation:

The one who states his case first seems right,
until the other comes and examines him. (Proverbs 18:17)

The first narrative can sound convincing — until the evidence arrives.

This contrast between words and works is important here. A narrative can be constructed quickly. A life, however, cannot be fabricated so easily. Over time, deeds accumulate into a pattern that either confirms or contradicts the story someone tells verbally about themselves.

That is why Jesus said:

By their fruits you will know them. (Matthew 7:16)

Fruit is slow evidence. It cannot be invented in a moment. The difference between Narrative testimony vs evidentiary testimony Narrative testimony = words about what happened. Evidentiary testimony = the pattern of what actually occurred. When the final account comes, evidence will outweigh narrative.

Some people attempt to testify in advance by controlling the story. They circulate their version of events, hoping that if the narrative takes hold, the truth will appear to confirm it. But narratives built on words alone cannot withstand the examination of time. A life eventually reveals what it truly contains. When the day of testing comes, explanations fade and the *works* themselves remain.

A man's life is his testimony.

Pre-testifying to control the narrative has a close parallel in Scripture with something called false witness.

In human settings, people sometimes attempt to manufacture testimony with words, hoping the narrative will shape the outcome before the truth is examined. That can happen when someone speaks falsely about another person, but it can also happen when someone constructs a version of themselves that is not true, hoping that the story will stand in place of the life.

Scripture treats this very seriously. The commandment is clear:

You shall not bear false witness against your neighbor.
(Exodus 20:16)

The reason this command is so strong is because testimony shapes judgment. If testimony is corrupted, justice itself is endangered. A person can try to bear false witness not only against another, but about himself—by presenting a version of his life that is more favorable than the truth. In human courts that can sometime work for a while. Words can confuse, mislead, and persuade.

But the Biblical idea of judgment removes that possibility, because the testimony does not depend on what a person says about himself. The testimony rests on what was actually done.

This is why Scripture repeatedly emphasizes works being revealed. When the record of a life is opened, the narrative someone has constructed will not be the decisive thing. The pattern of the life itself becomes the evidence.

The danger is real: a person may spend years trying to shape a story about what happened. But when the truth of a life is finally examined, stories cannot replace reality. In that sense, this warning is very sober. A person may control the narrative for a time, but he cannot ultimately control the testimony of the life he lived.

DREAM WITNESSES

What does a "witness" look like in a dream?

Silent, observant, note taking, there for the report, doesn't leave with the person or situation interviewed, stays with the report.

This chapter is to help you recall or in hindsight see: *Oh, that was a witness that was in my dream.*

When a dream contains a witness, the figure usually behaves differently from normal dream characters. They are not part of the emotional drama of the dream. They are there in a quiet, observational role.

Signs of a "Witness" Figure in a Dream:

1. Quiet Presence

A witness is often silent or speaks very little. They are not driving the action of the dream. They may simply stand nearby, watch what is happening, or observe the interaction between other people. Their silence is not passive; it feels intentional and attentive.

2. Observant, Not Participating

Unlike most dream figures, the witness does not get caught up in the situation. They typically do not argue, do not intervene, do not change the events. They observe what unfolds. The dreamer often senses that the person is paying careful attention.

3. Calm and Neutral

Witness figures often appear calm, composed, AND unemotional. They do not react strongly to the events taking place, even if the situation is intense. This neutrality can feel unusual in a dream.

4. Positioned Near the Dreamer

A witness frequently stands beside or slightly behind the dreamer. They are close enough to observe clearly, but they are not the central actor. This position resembles someone standing with you while something is being examined.

There's the feeling of being "noted." Sometimes the dreamer senses that the witness is mentally recording or noting what is happening. There may even be imagery suggesting writing, reading, reviewing, and looking at documents or records but sometimes the sense of record-keeping is simply felt, not seen.

They often do not leave with the dreamer. The witness may remain in the place where the events occurred, even when the dreamer moves on. This can create the impression that the witness is connected to the event or record, not to the dreamer personally.

They may appear ordinary. witnesses do not always look unusual. They may appear as an ordinary person, someone unknown, or someone the dreamer recognizes What distinguishes them is their role, not their appearance. They are aware of the whole situation. Even though they may say very little, the dreamer often senses that the witness understands exactly what is happening. There can be a quiet awareness that: *This person sees everything.*

In Scripture, important matters are often established by witnesses. The presence of a witness confirms that something has been seen and can be testified to.

A matter shall be established by the testimony of two or three witnesses. (Deuteronomy 19:15)

In dreams, a witness figure may symbolize that the events being shown are observed and recorded, not merely imagined.

If someone wonders whether a figure in their dream was acting as a witness, they might ask, *Was the person mostly watching rather than participating? Did they appear calm and observant? Did they seem to understand the situation without needing explanation? Did they remain connected to the place or event rather than following the dreamer?*

If several of these are true, the figure may be functioning symbolically as a witness.

A witness in a dream rarely dominates the scene. They stand quietly at the edge of the moment, seeing what is done and remembering it.

Please don't ignore your dreams; they are very telling.

Dreams should be inspired by and given by the Holy Spirit. There are manipulated dreams and evil dreams, and this is why you need Christian, Biblical interpretation so you can know the difference.

Now, the question is: *Why would God send a witness? Why is that witness in your dream? How or why is it that you can see them, or talk to them?*

God uses witnesses because Biblically, truth is confirmed through witnesses. The principle appears throughout the Bible: In the mouth of two or three witnesses shall every word be established. (2 Corinthians 13:1) The idea is that truth is not meant to stand on one voice alone. Witnesses confirm reality. When the Bible uses the language of witnesses, it often points to confirmation of truth, record of events, or testimony about actions.

A witness might appear in a dream. Dreams in Scripture sometimes communicate through symbolic roles—kings, messengers, shepherds, judges, witnesses. A "witness" in a dream can represent the idea that something in the dream matters enough to be observed or recorded. In other words, the presence of a witness can symbolize: this moment has significance, the event has testimony, and what is happening is being noted. Yes, God is watching, noting, keeping careful records. If a witness was *sent*, they were *sent* by God.

Did you pray about this matter? Did you ask God to specifically open up a case in the Courts of Heaven? This witness, sent by God could be part of the due diligence of the Highest Court on behalf of the truth in the matter that you have before the Lord.

GOD HEARS US WHEN WE PRAY. Amen.

The witness is not necessarily there to act; their presence emphasizes observation and testimony.

You might see or speak with them in the dream. Dreams often make abstract ideas visible. In waking life we don't see "testimony" or "record" as a person, but in dreams those concepts can appear as figures representing roles.

Seeing or interacting with such a figure could simply be the mind's way—or in a spiritual interpretation, the dream's symbolic language—of highlighting the role of witness or observer.

Scripture repeatedly uses witness imagery. People bear witness to events. A man's own conscience bears witness internally. God knows and records the truth of actions. This layered idea of testimony is why courtroom language appears so often in Biblical writing.

A man's life is his testimony. The presence of witnesses reinforces the idea that life itself becomes evidence.

In that sense, the witness in the dream could symbolize that events, choices, and actions have significance and testimony attached to them.

MONITORING SPIRITS & OTHERS

Many people see observing figures in dreams and assume they all mean the same thing, but in symbolic or Biblical-style dreams they can represent very different functions. Types of observing figures in dreams include the witness as we have already discussed. **A Witness** is connected to testimony.

A Messenger figure appears when information must be delivered. Characteristics are that they speak clearly or give instructions. They may deliver a warning or explanation often appears briefly and then leaves. The focus here is communication, not observation.

A Guide appears when the dream involves movement or direction. Typically they lead the dreamer somewhere. They may show a path or location, or they may explain what something means. The role is guidance, not testimony.

An Accuser. This type of figure appears in dreams where there is blame, accusation, condemnation, conflict over what happened. The atmosphere often feels tense or confrontational. Symbolically this can represent the role of accusation or internal conflict.

A Watcher / Observer. This figure is simply watching from a distance. Common traits: standing in shadows or in the background, not speaking, observing the dreamer rather than the event. This can symbolize awareness, scrutiny, or perception, depending on the dream's context.

A witness is not watching *you personally*. They are observing the event. They behave like someone in a courtroom who is present because something important is being established. Their role is to see, to remember, to testify. In many symbolic dreams involving testimony, there is the witness or witnesses. A witness does not have to be singular; they could be more than one, or many. I had a different dream where there was a stadium full of witnesses.

What is the difference between a witness and a "*monitoring spirit*'" in a dream?

The behaviors can look similar on the surface because both may appear watchful, but the nature, atmosphere, and function are very different.

Their purpose is to witness and gather information on their subject. A witness is present to observe and establish what has occurred. Their role relates to record, testimony, and confirmation. They are connected to truth and accountability. Scripturally, matters are established by witnesses. The witness exists so that what happens can be testified to accurately.

A *monitoring spirit,* in spiritual warfare language, is believed to be present to gather information for manipulation, accusation, or interference. Its goal is not truth but surveillance and exploitation. Instead of establishing truth, the intention is to use information against the person. In the dark kingdom a monitoring spirit is sent to find out the best way and day to attack a potential victim. The wicked lay in wait to attack the righteous. These attacks are not random, they are well planned; don't think they are not.

Atmosphere in the dream is often the clearest difference. Witness the atmosphere is usually calm, neutral, orderly, or observational. The witness may say little or nothing, but their presence does not feel invasive or threatening.

Often the dreamer senses clarity or seriousness, not disturbance. With a *monitoring spirit* the atmosphere often feels intrusive, suspicious, uneasy, and watchful in a predatory way. The dreamer may feel exposed, uncomfortable, followed, and studied. The tone is surveillance rather than observation.

Behavior of a witness: they stand quietly. They observe events. They do not interfere. They do not manipulate outcomes. They do not pursue the dreamer. Their role is simply to see and confirm.

The *monitoring spirit* is quite different. They may watch from hidden places. They may follow or track the dreamer. They may appear repeatedly in different dreams.

They may attempt to interact or influence events The behavior can feel covert or investigative.

They take different positions within the dream. The witness often stands beside the dreamer, near the event being observed, and calmly within the scene. They are usually openly present.

The *monitoring spirit o*ften appears at a distance, in shadows or corners, looking through windows or doorways, watching from concealed places. The presence can feel secretive or intrusive.

The witness is not there to pursue the dreamer personally. They are connected to the event or testimony, not to controlling the dreamer. They may even remain in the scene while the dreamer leaves.

Monitoring spirit -The attention feels directed at the dreamer themselves. The dreamer may feel followed, evaluated, or targeted.

Emotionally, dreamers often wake feeling thoughtful, reflective, sober, or calm. Even if the dream content was serious.

Monitoring Spirit - Dreamers often wake feeling uneasy, disturbed, watched, or unsettled. A Simple Way to Explain It to Readers. A witness observes what is happening so that the truth can later be testified to. A *monitoring spirit,* by contrast, watches in order to gather information for manipulation, accusation, oppression or attack. One is connected to testimony; the other to surveillance. Though both may appear watchful, the atmosphere surrounding them is very different.

Recap of witness in the dream: the person is calm and not part of the drama. A witness usually does not argue, chase, or act emotionally. They may stand nearby, watch quietly, walk with the dreamer but not lead, listen while events are explained. Their calmness often feels intentional, as if they are there to observe the facts. The witness very frequently appears during an explanation. The dreamer finds themselves explaining something, such as what happened, what someone did, why something occurred, what was taken, damaged, or altered. The witness listens carefully. They may nod or simply remain attentive.

This resembles giving testimony. The witness functions almost like someone who is receiving the report.

In the dream, the witness does not leave with the dreamer. This is one of the strongest clues. After the explanation or event is finished the dreamer moves on. Or, the scene changes; the dream shifts location. But the witness often remains in the place where the event occurred.

Why?

Because the witness is connected to the record of what happened, not to the dreamer personally. They are attached to the testimony, not the journey.

A witness in a dream rarely dominates the scene. They stand quietly at the edge of events, listening while the story unfolds. They do not interfere or argue. Their presence is calm and observant. When the moment passes, they often remain with the place where the events occurred, as if connected to the record rather than the traveler.

Witness figures in dreams often appear as ordinary people: a man in simple clothing, someone the dreamer does not know. It could be a neutral bystander, or a quiet official-looking person. They do not usually look dramatic or supernatural. What marks them is their role, not their appearance.

There are four dream symbols that often appear when a dream is about testimony or records (things like books, files, rooms, and certain types of buildings). They appear surprisingly often in dreams that involve accountability or truth being examined.

In dreams dealing with testimony, accountability, or records, certain symbols appear again and again. They are almost like the visual language of a report being taken. Four that show up frequently include: books, ledgers, files, folders, medical charts, written reports, and or documents being examined. These objects symbolize that events are being recorded or reviewed.

Dreams involving testimony often occur in places where records are normally kept. Examples: offices, reception areas, administrative rooms, hospitals, government buildings, and courtrooms. These locations symbolize order, review, and accountability.

In testimony dreams, the dreamer often finds themselves explaining something that happened. Someone is listening while the story is told. The listener may be silent, attentive, thoughtful and or mentally noting details. The atmosphere often feels serious but calm, like a report is being taken. This mirrors the role of a witness or recorder.

After testimony is given, the dream often moves toward a door, a hallway, an elevator, stairs, or leaving the building. These symbols indicate the completion of the report and movement to the next phase.

When several of these elements appear together, the dream may be structured like a testimony event: A setting where records exist. Evidence or documents involved. Someone observing or listening. The dreamer explaining events. Departure or transition afterward. That structure mirrors the process of giving an account.

Some dreams unfold like testimony being given. The setting often resembles a place where records are kept. Documents or files appear. Someone listens quietly as the story is told. When the explanation is complete, the dreamer moves on, leaving the scene as though the report has been received.

Back to my dream: there were birds in the hallway. In my dream, I encountered several birds while walking toward the elevator to leave the building. Recall there was at least one of each, a grayish white pigeon-like bird, a darker pigeon, and a murky gray-green bird with an unusual square face. They were on the floor, moving about, and I had to walk around them.

Birds in dreams can symbolize many things depending on context, but when they appear watching, gathered, or positioned along a path, they can represent observers or messengers connected to events being witnessed. In Scripture, birds sometimes represent watchful presence or beings that observe what is happening in the Earth. But another important detail here is their location. They were in the hallway between the place of testimony and the exit.

That suggests something interesting: the moment of testimony had passed, and as I was leaving the scene, the hallway contained watchers along the path of departure. I had to navigate around them, but they did not attack or interfere. They simply existed in the space as observers. Symbolically, that resembles *beings* present along the path of life who see what happens.

> Seeing we also are compassed about with so great a cloud of witnesses, let us lay aside every weight… and let us run with patience the race that is set before us.
> (Hebrews 12:1)

The writer of Hebrews says Believers are surrounded by a cloud of witnesses as they run their race. These witnesses testify to faithfulness. Based on my dream, this could suggest: a witness observing the testimony. a record-related environment (the office, charts, server). a departure path (hallway and elevator), with watchers along the path (the birds). Dear Readers: Life unfolds in the presence of witnesses.

We all live in the presence of witnesses. The idea of witnesses surrounding human life is found repeatedly in Scripture. Witnesses include: those who have gone before in faith, the testimony of righteous lives, heavenly observers, and the record of deeds themselves. The implication is not meant to create fear but accountability and encouragement.

Life is not hidden. Actions matter. Faithfulness is seen.

W are surrounded by a great cloud of witnesses; life is not lived in isolation. Actions, decisions, and faithfulness are observed and recorded in ways we do not always see. A person may imagine that their life is private, but the testimony of that life unfolds before witnesses both visible and unseen.

If a person's life is observed and recorded along the way, then the final accounting is not a sudden interrogation. It is the revealing of a testimony that has been witnessed all along. A man's life is his testimony. When the time comes to plead the case, the witnesses and the works will already be present.

A WATCHER OR A WATCHMAN

What's the difference between a 'watcher' and a "watchman"?

A Watcher. The word *watcher* appears in the Bible in a very specific place: the Book of Daniel. In Daniel's vision we read:

> I saw in the visions of my head upon my bed, and behold a watcher and a holy one came down from heaven. (Daniel 4:13)

A watcher in this context refers to a Heavenly being that observes human affairs and carries out Divine decrees. Key characteristics of a watcher is that they are a Heavenly observer. They are sent from Heaven. They are involved with Divine Judgment or decrees. They watch the affairs of men, but, they are not part of human society.

In Daniel's case, the watcher announced the judgment that would come upon Nebuchadnezzar. So, a watcher is essentially an observer connected to the Heavenly Court.

A watchman, by contrast, is a human role.

In ancient cities, watchmen stood on the walls or towers to look for danger or approaching events. Their job was to warn the people. The prophet Ezekiel describes this clearly.

> Son of man, I have made thee a watchman unto the house of Israel: therefore hear the word at my mouth, and give them warning from me. (Ezekiel 3:17)

Key characteristics of a watchman: they are a human servant of God. They are positioned to observe what is coming. They are responsible to warn others. And, they are accountable if they fail to speak. So, the watchman is not merely observing; he is tasked with alerting people to danger or truth.

The core difference can be summarized simply. A Watcher is a Heavenly observer, part of the Divine Court. They observe and sometimes announces decrees.

The watchman is a **human** servant who is stationed to guard or warn. They are responsible to speak when danger appears.

In relation to testimony, a watcher observes events and confirms what has occurred. A watchman sees danger or truth approaching and sounds the warning. A watcher observes what happens, but a watchman is responsible to warn what is coming. One sees and records; the other sees and speaks.

THE ACCUSER (THE PETITION)

In the Book of Revelation we see the role of accusation:

> For the accuser of our brethren is cast down, which accused them before our God day and night. (Revelation 12:10)

An accusation is essentially a petition brought before the court. A petition alone does not determine the outcome. Evidence is examined. Witnesses are sent and testify. Works are revealed. The books are opened. Deeds are inspected. Works are tried.

> Every man's work shall be made manifest… and the fire shall try every man's work of what sort it is. (1 Corinthians)

The accusation does not stand alone. The Court examines the substance of the life. Before we had an Advocate the accusations would have all stuck. The Accuser brings charges (Revelation 12:10). The accusation is most often true, based on real failures, sins, or wrongdoing. Therefore, the accusation has substance.

The Law Established the Standard before Christ's redemptive work, the law defined righteousness and exposed violations.

By the law is the knowledge of sin. (Romans 3:20)

Without intervention, the charge stands. But we are no longer standing there alone; thank You, Jesus.

If any man sin, we have an advocate with the Father, Jesus Christ the righteous. (1 John 2:1)

Our Advocate does not pretend the charge never existed. Instead, the Advocate addresses the charge. In Christian theology this happens through forgiveness, atonement through the Blood of Jesus, and by reconciliation.

Once Our Advocate is present, the courtroom dynamic changes. It is no longer accusation going straight to verdict. It becomes: Accusation, Our Defense, and then a Righteous Judgment. The Advocate introduces the possibility of Mercy and restoration. We will see this in the Courts of Heaven as well as in just human courts.

There are still corrupt courts in the seen and unseen worlds that operate under their own "law." This is why seen or unseen, all of us should stay prayed up and plead the Blood of Jesus because Jesus, His Blood, His Righteousness, and the Mercy and Grace of God can save us even in what looks like impossible situations.

The accusation does not stand alone. The Court of Heaven examines the substance of the life. Accusations may exist, but they are not the only evidence. The whole life—its actions, responses, and transformations—forms the record that is considered.

The Judgment of the Court. Ultimately the throne renders the decision. Daniel's vision describes it like this:

> The court was seated, and the books were opened.
> (Daniel 7:10)

People often focus on the accusation, but the process also involves witnesses observing, works being revealed, testimony established, and the Advocate, not the accused responding.

Order in the Court! If you are in the Courts of Heaven, your plea is ALWAYS guilty. Your Advocate is always Jesus Christ; do not try to represent yourself. Your defense is ALWAYS the Blood of Jesus.

Because we now have a Great Advocate, the Courtroom is not merely a place of accusation, but it is also a place where truth is examined fully.

Many people live as though life is private and unnoticed. Biblical imagery suggests something different. Life unfolds before witnesses. Actions accumulate into testimony. Accusations may be brought, but the record of the life is fully examined.

A man's life is his testimony.

LEARNING THE COURTROOM IN SMALL MATTERS

Saints of God, know this: Pleading your case is about daily or intermittent life issues **as well as** the whole big picture, when it is all said and done. This is so we get to understand it *in part* first -- if we are paying attention. Accountability is not only a final event but an ongoing process. Life gives us smaller moments of examination long before the final accounting. If a person is attentive, they begin to understand the process *in part* before they ever see it in full.

Scripture hints at this pattern when Jesus said,

> For there is nothing covered, that shall not be revealed; neither hid, that shall not be known. (Luke 12:2)

That revealing often begins in small ways throughout a person's life. Situations arise where truth surfaces, motives are exposed, and actions produce consequences. Those moments function almost like miniature hearings, where a person begins to see what their life is producing.

When someone "pleads their case" in daily life, several things often occur. An accusation arises; someone says something happened. Facts are examined — what actually occurred? Witnesses may exist; others saw or experienced the event. Evidence appears as actions, words, patterns. A conclusion forms. Right or wrong, a correction, or vindication will be the judgment in the end. This is why we have human courts, mediation, and the like.

These moments are smaller versions of the larger process of accountability. A person who pays attention begins to see patterns such as truth eventually surfaces. Narratives do not always hold. Actions produce consequences. Character becomes visible over time. Through those experiences, a person learns how Truth operates.

Through life's events, we may begin to get partial understanding before the full picture. In many areas of life, we understand something first in part.

For now we see through a glass, darkly; but then face to face. (1 Corinthians 13:12)

The idea is that we grasp pieces of the reality now, and those pieces prepare us to understand the full reality later. Daily situations where truth is revealed or tested can serve as early lessons in discernment. Smart people pay attention. People who reflect on these experiences begin to recognize that life itself is teaching them what truth looks like, how evidence works, how actions accumulate into testimony. We begin to see how character is revealed.

God knows who we are right now, the revelation of our character is for us, not God. We can see if we are converting, transforming, becoming more like Christ or remaining in our flesh.

Those lessons can shape how a person lives.

Instead of assuming that words alone define reality, they begin to understand that life itself becomes the evidence. The final accounting of a life is not the first time truth is examined. Throughout life there are smaller moments where motives are exposed, actions are weighed, and outcomes reveal what was really built. If a person pays attention, these moments become lessons in how testimony works. We begin to understand the process in part long before the full record is opened.

The testimony of a life is being written long before the day it is examined.

GOOD OR BAD -- GOOD *AND* BAD

Human life unfolds in the presence of witnesses, before God, and within a moral universe where actions matter. Good or bad—good and bad—we are never alone. A person may imagine that life is private, that decisions are made in isolation and disappear into the past. But Scripture suggests otherwise. Our lives unfold before God, and our actions become part of a testimony that does not simply vanish. Choices leave traces. Deeds accumulate. Truth eventually comes into the light.

We are surrounded by so great a cloud of witnesses (Hebrews). That image does not suggest surveillance meant to frighten, but rather a reminder that life is lived within a larger story. Faithfulness is seen. Perseverance matters. The race is run in the presence of those who have gone before and before the One who judges rightly. Every moment carries weight. The quiet acts of integrity, the hidden struggles, the choices no one else notices—none of them are meaningless. They become part of the testimony of a life.

A man's life is his testimony, and that good or bad—good and bad—we are never alone. There are no secrets; not really. Every decision leaves its mark. Every word carries weight. Every act of faithfulness or compromise becomes part of the record of a life.

Life is not lived in isolation, even if you live on an island. It unfolds in the presence of those who have gone before, before Heaven itself, and before the One who sees all things clearly. If you get the attention of the dark kingdom, your life may be lived out in front of *monitoring spirits* whose goal is to report what you do to the Accuser who will report what you do as an evil petition before the Throne of God.

For that reason, even the smallest choices matter, as they will become part of the testimony a life will one day present.

Good or bad—good and bad—we are never alone.

So many men want to live and stay young and are elated the next morning when they wake up again so they can live! But our deepest joy and satisfaction may be to wake up in the morning alive so we have another chance to get it right on this side. On the side where we are still involved in the writing of the books where it is written of us. Those books are the ones that will be open ultimately. Are there things you want to change in yours? Rewrites, not just strikeovers. Only the Blood of Jesus can blot out what has already been recorded. On this side, we can work toward that, because in the end, the life itself will speak; a man's life is his testimony.

LIFE IS SPEAKING

Life is already speaking. Maybe it only counts when a person gets to the age of accountability? Things we say, things we do create **patterns**. Those patterns ***speak***. They speak to us and urge us to repeat, or they teach us and urge us, *Don't do that again*.

They speak to people who are related to us who either want to be just like us or nothing like us. They speak to others who say, Oh, that's so-and-so, we know exactly what they will do... It can't be prejudice if what is thought about you comes from you, and not from people like you, or 'your family', but actually YOU and your own track record. Your life is already speaking.

In many ways, life begins speaking long before a person ever thinks about judgment or accountability. The testimony is forming in real time.

Patterns of life become evidence.

Life is already speaking.

A person does not suddenly begin building a testimony at the end of life. The testimony begins the moment choices begin to form patterns. Words spoken repeatedly, actions taken again and again, habits formed over time—these things gather into a record.

Patterns develop. Those patterns begin to speak. They speak to the person themselves. Some patterns urge us to repeat them. Others teach us painful lessons and quietly warn us, *Do not do that again.*

A life establishes its own reputation. Long before the final accounting ever occurs, the testimony is already being written. And it is already being heard.

By their fruits you will know them. (Matthew 7:16)

Fruit does not appear all at once. It grows from patterns of life. Over time it becomes unmistakable.

Your life is already speaking. There are really two testimonies operating in a person's life. One is the story people tell. The other is the pattern their life produces. Those two things do not always agree.

Life is already speaking. Some people spend a great deal of energy trying to control the narrative about their lives. They explain their actions, defend their motives, reinterpret their decisions, and offer their version of events before anyone else can speak.

In this way they attempt to testify in advance. But words are not the strongest testimony. Patterns are. Choices are. Habits are. A life lived over time produces evidence. Choices repeated become habits. Habits repeated become character. Character repeated becomes reputation.

Soon people begin to say, *That is who that person is.* Not because of rumor or prejudice, but because the evidence has accumulated.

The life itself has spoken. This is why narratives cannot ultimately overcome reality. A person may try to explain their life, but the pattern of that life continues to speak long after the explanation ends.

The testimony is already in progress. Your testimony is already in progress. So is mine. The truth is that it has been speaking all along.

Your life is already speaking. The evidence is already being entered into the record. Every day it adds another line to the testimony. The evidence is already being entered into the record.

Good or bad—good and bad—the results of our choices do not disappear like a fallen video character that disintegrates and then dissolves, leaving no evidence behind. Life does not reset.

Words spoken remain spoken, except by the Grace of God where we may renounce wrong things spoken. Actions taken remain part of the story, unless they are repented of and most of the time, quickly and not repeated. Patterns formed continue to shape the future.

Even when the moment passes, the effects of that moment continue. Choices leave marks on character, on relationships, and on reputation. Over time those marks accumulate into the testimony of a life. Nothing simply vanishes unless we ask God to wash it away, cleanse us, consecrate us, make us new.

Else, the record continues to grow.

Every day another line is added to the testimony, and the evidence is quietly entered into the record. Life is not a game that resets. It is a testimony that accumulates.

THE VOLUME OF THE BOOK

You, me, and all of us humans, are so powerful that everything you do and say is important, recorded, and does not disappear. Ever. There is a volume that is written of a person and in this life, we are allowed the Grace to co-write it. That life is our own.

> Every idle word that men shall speak, they shall give account thereof in the day of judgment. (Matthew 12:36)

Not because humans are meant to live in fear, but because life has significance. Choices matter. Actions matter. Words matter.

> Lo, I come: in the volume of the book it is written of me. (Psalm 40:7)

All the days of a life are known to God.

> In thy book all my members were written, which in continuance were fashioned, when as yet there was none of them. (Psalm 139:16)

Put together, these ideas suggest something remarkable. There is a story of a life, and the person living that life participates in how that story unfolds. We are given the Grace of participation, even having free will.

Life is not mechanical or predetermined like a script we cannot influence. Instead opportunities appear, choices are made, character forms, patterns develop, and then testimony grows.

Each day adds another page.

There is a volume written concerning every life. The pages are not empty, and they do not vanish when the day is over. Words spoken, actions taken, and choices repeated become lines in the testimony of a person. Yet there is Grace in the process. We are not merely characters reading a script—we are participants in how the story unfolds. Each day offers another opportunity to write well.

Your life is already speaking.

THE RECORD

The Scriptures speak often of witnesses, but they also speak of something closely related: **records**. If witnesses confirm what has happened, records preserve it. The Bible repeatedly refers to books that exist that contain the story of human lives, the memory of events, and the testimony of what has been done. These passages reveal that the Court of God does not depend on fading human memory. Truth is preserved in a record that cannot ultimately be altered or erased.

These words are later quoted in the book of Hebrews and applied to Christ, revealing that even the life and mission of the Messiah were written in the Divine record long before they unfolded in history.

The idea is profound. A life does not appear suddenly in the moment of judgment. Its story has already been written, line by line, through the unfolding of events. Scripture returns to this image again and again.

The prophet Daniel described a vision in which the Court of Heaven was assembled. Thrones were set in place, the Ancient of Days took His seat, and countless witnesses stood before Him. Daniel writes that the court was seated and the books were opened (Daniel 7:10)

Those books represent the preserved testimony of lives and events. They are the record of what has happened—what people have done, how they have lived, what choices they have made. The same image appears again in the book of Revelation, where John describes the final judgment of humanity.

> And I saw the dead, small and great, standing before God, and books were opened… and the dead were judged according to their works, by the things which were written in the books. (Revelation 20:12)

These passages remind us that God's justice rests on truth that has been recorded. Nothing is forgotten. Nothing is lost. What has been done in secret remains known before Him. Yet the record spoken of in Scripture is not only a record of wrongdoing. It also preserves faithfulness, devotion, repentance, and acts of quiet obedience that may have gone unnoticed by the world.

The prophet Malachi describes a moment when people who feared the Lord spoke with one another about Him. The passage says:

> A book of remembrance was written before Him for those who feared the Lord and who meditate on His name. (Malachi 3:16)

Even a conversation about God became part of the record. This reveals something remarkable about the nature of the record before Heaven. It does not merely catalog failure. It remembers faithfulness. It preserves what is good.

Every act of obedience, every moment of integrity, every quiet decision to walk in truth becomes part of a testimony that cannot be erased. When we understand this, the idea of giving an account before God begins to look different.

Many people imagine the final judgment as a moment when they must suddenly explain their entire lives. Scriptures suggest something deeper. The account has been forming all along. Day by day, the story of a life is written. Choices become lines in the record. Decisions shape the testimony. Faithfulness becomes part of a story that cannot be altered once it has been lived. In this sense, the Believer is not waiting until the end of life to present a defense. The testimony is already being written.

This is why integrity matters even when no one else appears to be watching. This is why faithfulness matters even in small decisions that seem insignificant. Each one becomes part of the record. And when the books are opened, the story of a life will already be there.

For those who belong to Christ, that record will not stand alone. The advocacy of Christ stands with it. Redemption is written into the story. Grace is woven into the record. But the life that was lived will still testify. Because in the Court of God, a life does not appear suddenly at the moment of judgment. It arrives already written. In the *volume* of the book.

WHEN THE RECORD IS ATTACKED

If truth is preserved in a record, it should not surprise us that there are times when people attempt to alter that record.

Throughout history, one of the most common strategies used against truth has been the effort to distort what actually happened. Sometimes this is done through accusation. Sometimes it is done through rumor or slander. At other times, it happens more quietly, through the rearranging of facts or the selective recall of events.

In every generation there are moments when the story of a situation is retold in a way that no longer resembles the truth. What was done is questioned. What was said is reinterpreted. What actually happened becomes difficult for others to see.

The Bible is not silent about this reality. Scripture repeatedly shows that the record of events can be challenged, misunderstood, or even deliberately misrepresented in the courts of men.

Joseph experienced this when he was falsely accused in Egypt. His actions were interpreted in a way that was completely opposite of the truth. The result was imprisonment and years of waiting before the record of his life was understood correctly.

David faced similar distortions when Saul turned public opinion against him. Though David had served faithfully, he was suddenly portrayed as a threat to the kingdom. Rumors and accusations spread quickly, shaping a narrative that did not reflect the truth of David's character.

The prophet Jeremiah also experienced the same pattern. Those who rejected his message sought to discredit him personally, hoping that if they could undermine the messenger, they could dismiss the message. These examples remind us that the record of a life is often contested in the court of public opinion.

Human systems are imperfect. They are influenced by emotion, loyalty, fear, and misunderstanding. People may repeat information they have never verified. Stories may evolve as they are passed from one person to another. In such an environment, it is possible for the appearance of truth to become separated from truth itself.

This is why the Scriptures continually point believers back to the Court of God.

While human narratives may shift, the divine record does not change. What has truly happened remains known before Him.

You number my wanderings; put my tears into Your bottle; are they not in Your book?" (Psalm 56:8)

The image is deeply personal. Even the tears of a person's life are remembered by God. Nothing that happens within a life disappears into forgetfulness. Because of this, attempts to distort the record ultimately fail in the presence of Divine Truth.

This does not mean that distortion never causes temporary harm. Joseph spent years in prison before the truth of his character was recognized. David spent long seasons fleeing from Saul's pursuit. Jeremiah endured rejection and suffering because many refused to believe his words.

Yet in each case the same pattern eventually emerged. The truth remained. The record of a life lived before God continued to speak, even when circumstances seemed to contradict it.

Over time, what was hidden became visible. Joseph was raised from prison to leadership because his wisdom and integrity could not be denied. David was eventually recognized as the rightful king. Jeremiah's words proved true when the events he had foretold came to pass. The record stood.

For the Believer today, this principle offers both comfort and instruction. There will be moments when the narrative surrounding a situation does not reflect reality. There may be seasons when the truth seems buried beneath misunderstanding or accusation. During such times the temptation is strong to fight every claim, correct every rumor, and force the world to acknowledge what is true. But the Scriptures remind us that the ultimate defense of a life does not rest solely in immediate vindication. It rests in the record that exists before God.

When a person lives with integrity, the testimony of that life continues to accumulate evidence over time. Decisions made in private, faithfulness demonstrated in difficulty, and character revealed through consistent conduct all become part of a record that cannot be permanently erased.

Eventually that record begins to speak for itself. Truth has a quiet endurance that falsehood lacks. While lies must constantly be reinforced to survive, truth possesses a stability that allows it to stand when examined. For this reason the believer is called to remain faithful even when the surrounding narrative appears confused or hostile.

Integrity today becomes evidence tomorrow. Faithfulness today becomes witness later. The record continues to grow. And when the Court of God examines the matter, that record will speak clearly. In the end, while people may attempt to challenge the story of a life, they cannot erase the testimony written before God; The record remains.

THE COURT OF PUBLIC OPINION

Not every court operates according to truth.

Long before a matter ever reaches a place of careful examination, it is often tried in another court altogether—the court of public opinion. This court does not require evidence. It does not wait for witnesses. It rarely pauses long enough to examine the full record. Instead, it moves quickly, driven by perception, emotion, and the influence of voices that shape the narrative.

In this court, a story can travel farther than the truth before anyone has the opportunity to question it. A rumor repeated often enough begins to sound convincing. A suspicion shared widely enough begins to feel like fact.

By the time the truth emerges, the judgment of the crowd may already have been formed.

Scripture gives many examples of this kind of court.

Joseph experienced it when Potiphar's household accepted an accusation against him without investigation. His reputation was decided by the testimony of a single voice, and the result was imprisonment.

David experienced it when Saul persuaded the nation that David was a threat. Though David had served faithfully and fought for the kingdom, the narrative surrounding him shifted. Suspicion replaced gratitude, and the crowd's perception changed almost overnight.

Even the Son of God was not immune to this court. When Jesus stood before the crowd during His trial, the voices of accusation were loud and insistent. The same people who had once welcomed Him into Jerusalem soon shouted for His crucifixion. The court of public opinion had reached its verdict long before the truth was fully considered.

These examples reveal something important about the nature of public judgment. The crowd is often guided not by careful examination but by the momentum of a story. Once a narrative gains strength, it becomes difficult for people to question it. Many prefer the comfort of agreement with the crowd rather than the effort required to examine the facts for themselves.

This is why the court of public opinion can feel so overwhelming. Its judgments are swift. Its conclusions are loud. And its memory is often short. Yet Scripture repeatedly reminds believers that this court is not the one that ultimately decides the truth.

Human opinion is temporary. Narratives change. Crowds move on to the next story. If your business has ever been out in the streets, then you know what I'm talking about.

The Court of God, however, operates differently. God is not influenced by the momentum of a rumor or the pressure of a crowd. His judgment does not depend on how widely a story has spread or how strongly people feel about it. He examines the record. He considers the witnesses. He knows the truth of what has occurred.

Because of this, the Believer must learn to live with a perspective that reaches beyond the shifting judgments of public opinion. There will be moments when the crowd misunderstands. There will be times when the story told about a situation does not reflect the reality of what happened. These seasons can be painful, especially when reputation and relationships are affected.

Scriptures call Believers to anchor their confidence somewhere deeper than public approval. Paul once wrote that it meant very little to him how he was judged by human courts. He understood that the final examination of his life belonged to the Lord. That perspective freed him from the exhausting need to win every argument before people. Paul still spoke truth. He still defended the Gospel when necessary. But he did not measure his life by the approval or disapproval of the crowd.

He measured it by faithfulness before God. This is an important lesson for anyone seeking to live with integrity. If a person builds their sense of identity on the opinions of others, they will constantly be pushed and pulled by the changing winds of public judgment. Praise one day may turn into criticism the next.

A life anchored in truth does not need the constant validation of the crowd. It needs only the confidence that comes from knowing that the record before God is accurate. Public opinion may rise and fall. Narratives may change. But the testimony of a life lived before God continues to stand.

When the books are opened, the Court that matters most will not be the one that shouted the loudest. It will be the one that judges according to truth.

SILENCE BEFORE THE JUDGE

Order in the Court; silence!

There are moments in every case when words are expected. Accusations have been made. Questions are raised. Voices demand explanation. In such moments the natural impulse is to respond immediately—to defend oneself, to correct the narrative, and to explain what really happened. The instinct to speak is powerful because silence can feel like surrender. Yet Scripture reveals something surprising.

There are times when the strongest response is **silence**. Not the silence of defeat, but the silence of confidence in a Higher Court. The most striking example of this appears in the life of Jesus. When He stood before those who accused Him, the charges were severe and the atmosphere was hostile. False witnesses came forward. Stories were twisted. Motives were questioned.

Yet the Gospels record that Jesus often answered very little. Before Pilate and the chief priests, He spoke only a few words. At times He said nothing at all. The silence puzzled those who watched. Pilate himself marveled that Jesus did not defend Himself more forcefully against the accusations being brought against Him.

Jesus understood something that many people struggle to grasp. He knew that the truth of His life did not depend on the arguments of the moment. The record already existed. Everything He had done—every word He had spoken, every act of compassion, every demonstration of authority—had already testified to who He was. The accusations could not erase that record.

In the same way, the prophets and servants of God throughout Scripture often endured seasons in which their words were rejected or misunderstood. Jeremiah spoke truth faithfully, yet many refused to believe him. David endured accusations from Saul even though his loyalty to the king had been proven repeatedly.

In such moments the temptation is often to continue arguing until the other side finally admits the truth. But this rarely happens. When a person is determined to believe a particular narrative, additional arguments often only deepen the conflict. Words multiply, but understanding does not necessarily follow.

This is why Scripture sometimes points believers toward restraint. Silence does not mean that truth is abandoned. Instead, it reflects confidence that the truth does not need constant defense to remain true.

A life lived faithfully continues to speak even when the person themselves says very little.

The Book of Proverbs captures this principle when it reminds us that a person's conduct eventually reveals their character. What someone consistently does over time carries more weight than a single moment of explanation.

In the court of public opinion, silence can feel dangerous. People may interpret it in many different ways. Some may assume that silence indicates weakness or guilt. In the Court of God, silence can reflect something very different.

It can reflect trust.

Trust that the Judge sees what others do not see. Trust that the record of a life is already known before Him. Trust that truth does not disappear simply because it is not argued loudly.

This does not mean that Believers should never speak when accused. There are moments when clarification is necessary and when truth must be expressed plainly. The apostles themselves spoke boldly when defending the message of the Gospel. Scripture also shows that Wisdom sometimes rests in knowing when words will no longer advance the truth. At that point, continued argument becomes less about Justice and more about noise.

Silence can then become a form of testimony in itself. It declares that the believer's confidence rests not in winning every debate but in the integrity of the life that has been lived before God.

Over time, that integrity begins to answer the accusations on its own.

People who observe closely begin to recognize patterns. The consistency of a life becomes difficult to dismiss. What once seemed uncertain becomes clearer as the evidence accumulates.

Truth, when allowed to stand long enough, reveals itself. For this reason, the Believer who understands the Court of God does not feel compelled to control every conversation or correct every misunderstanding immediately. Instead, he continues to live faithfully. He continues to walk uprightly. He continues to trust that the Judge who sees all things will eventually bring truth to light.

When the final judgment comes, the decisive question will not be who argued the most convincingly in the moment. The question will be what the record of a life actually shows. In that Court, the testimony of a life lived in truth will speak louder than any defense that words could provide.

THE WITNESS OF A LIFE

Every court depends on testimony. Witnesses step forward, speak what they have seen, and confirm what is true. Their words help establish the facts of a case. Without witnesses, the court is left with claims that cannot easily be verified. But the Scriptures reveal that testimony does not always come from a single moment of speech. Often it comes from something much larger and more powerful.

It comes from the pattern of a life. Over time, the choices a person makes begin to form a consistent story. Actions repeated day after day create a record that becomes difficult to dispute. Character, when observed long enough, reveals itself. This is why the Bible places such emphasis on the way a person lives.

Apostle Peter urged Believers to conduct themselves honorably among those around them. His reason was simple: when people observe a life marked by integrity, that life becomes a witness to the truth.

A person's conduct begins to speak. It speaks in moments of pressure when integrity would be easy to abandon. It speaks in quiet decisions made when no one else appears to be watching. It speaks in the consistency of a life that refuses to compromise its values even when circumstances are difficult.

Over time, these choices accumulate into something powerful. They become evidence.

A single act of integrity may be overlooked, but years of integrity create a testimony that cannot easily be dismissed. A single moment of faithfulness may seem small, but a lifetime of faithfulness builds a record that speaks clearly when examined. This is why Scripture repeatedly encourages believers to remain steadfast in their conduct. The goal is the formation of a testimony. The story of a life is being written every day. Each decision adds another line to that story. Each act of obedience strengthens the witness of that life.

In the moment, many of these choices may seem ordinary. They may appear too small to matter in the larger picture of a person's life. Yet when viewed together, they form a pattern that reveals who a person truly is. This is how a life becomes a witness.

The court of public opinion may change quickly. Narratives may shift as new voices emerge. Rumors may rise and fall with the passing of time, but the consistent testimony of a life remains. People who observe over many years begin to see what is genuine. They recognize patterns that cannot easily be fabricated. Integrity demonstrated repeatedly becomes difficult to deny.

Eventually, the life itself answers the questions that once seemed complicated.

Paul expressed this idea when he spoke of Believers as ***living letters,*** known and read by those around them. Their lives communicated something about the truth of the Gospel long before many people heard it explained. In the same way, the life of a Believer becomes a visible testimony of what it means to walk with God.

This is why the final judgment described in Scripture does not rely solely on spoken arguments. The books that are opened contain the story of what has actually been lived. The record of a life is already there. For the Believer, this truth carries both responsibility and encouragement. It reminds us that every decision matters. The choices we make today contribute to the testimony that our lives will eventually present; you are currently pleading your case, that will be the answers that you will give later. Faithfulness in small things becomes part of a larger record that reveals who we truly are.

At the same time, it offers reassurance. The believer does not need to construct a defense through clever words when the time comes to stand before God. The testimony of a life lived in truth will already exist. The pattern of integrity, the moments of obedience, the quiet acts of faithfulness—all of these will speak. In that moment, the most powerful witness will be the life that has been lived across many years. In the Court of God, a man's life is not merely observed; it becomes his testimony; that is how that man will plead his case.

THE RECORD OF FAITHFULNESS

When people think about judgment, they often imagine a record filled only with failure. They picture a list of mistakes, sins, and missteps waiting to be examined. The idea can feel heavy, as though the record of a life exists only to expose what went wrong. Scriptures reveal something far more hopeful.

The record kept before God does not preserve only wrongdoing. It also preserves **faithfulness**.

Throughout the Bible we find reminders that God remembers the quiet acts of obedience that others may never notice. The smallest decisions made in faith are not lost. The moments of integrity that pass unseen by the world are not forgotten.

The prophet Malachi describes a beautiful scene that illustrates this truth.

Then those who feared the Lord spoke to one another,
and the Lord listened and heard them;
so a book of remembrance was written before Him
for those who feared the Lord
and who meditate on His name. (Malachi 3:16)

In that passage, people simply spoke together about the Lord. There was no dramatic event, no public display, no extraordinary miracle. Yet the Scripture tells us that God listened and that a **Book of Remembrance** was written. Even a conversation about Him became part of the record, revealing something profound about the heart of God. The Divine record is not merely a ledger of human failure. It is also a remembrance of devotion.

A decision to remain honest when dishonesty would be easier becomes part of the testimony. A moment of compassion shown to someone in need becomes part of the record. A quiet prayer offered in a difficult season becomes part of the story of a life lived before God.

Many of these moments pass without recognition from the world. No one writes about them. No audience applauds them. Often the person who acts faithfully may feel as though their obedience disappears into the ordinary flow of life. Yet before God, none of it is lost.

The Scriptures remind us again and again that God sees what others overlook. Jesus spoke of this when He encouraged His followers not to practice righteousness merely for public attention. Acts of generosity, prayer, and devotion done in secret were not wasted, He said, because the Father who sees in secret remembers.

Faithfulness that escapes human recognition is still fully known before God. This truth offers deep encouragement for anyone who has wondered whether their quiet obedience matters. The world tends to celebrate visible accomplishments and dramatic achievements. But the kingdom of God measures life differently.

In the Kingdom of Heaven, consistency matters. The daily decision to walk in truth matters. The perseverance that continues to trust God in difficult seasons matters. All of these moments become part of the testimony written in the record of a life. When the Scriptures speak of the books being opened, they remind us that God's memory is perfect. He does not forget what the world has overlooked.

The hours spent serving others. The sacrifices made for the sake of integrity. The prayers whispered in moments of uncertainty. Each one is remembered.

This also helps us understand something important about the justice of God. Judgment is not a narrow examination of isolated mistakes. It is the consideration of an entire life—the full story, including both weakness and faithfulness.

For those who belong to Christ, the record of faithfulness is woven together with the Grace of redemption. Failures are not ignored, but they are met with forgiveness. Weakness is not the final word, because the transforming work of God becomes part of the story. What remains is the testimony of a life shaped by Grace.

Over time, this testimony becomes clearer.

A life that continues to choose integrity, even when it is costly, reveals something real. A person who continues to trust God through difficulty demonstrates a faith that cannot easily be dismissed. These choices form a witness that grows stronger with time. They become the quiet evidence that a life has been lived before God.

When the final account is examined, that faithfulness will not be forgotten. The record will show it. In the court of God, faithfulness—no matter how small it may seem in the moment—is always remembered.

A MAN'S LIFE IS HIS TESTIMONY

Every case eventually reaches a moment when the judge examines the evidence. Witnesses have spoken. Records have been presented. Arguments have been made. At that point, the question becomes simple: *What does the evidence show?*

In the Court of God, the most powerful evidence is not a single statement spoken in a moment of defense. It is the accumulated record of a life.

This is why Scripture places such emphasis on the way a person lives. The choices made over many years form a pattern that reveals the truth about a person's character. Words may persuade for a moment, but the consistency of a life cannot easily be fabricated.

Over time, life itself becomes testimony.

The Bible repeatedly points to this reality. Jesus taught that a tree is known by its fruit. The nature of the tree is revealed not by its claims, but by what it consistently produces. In the same way, a person's life reveals what is within the heart.

A single action may not tell the whole story. Anyone can experience a moment of weakness or make a mistake. But when the choices of a life are viewed together, they form a pattern that becomes unmistakable. Faithfulness produces one kind of record. Deception produces another. The pattern tells the truth.

This is why accusations alone cannot determine the outcome of a case before God. Accusations may raise questions, but they cannot override the testimony of a life that has been lived with integrity.

Over time, the evidence accumulates.

The decisions made in private begin to form a public witness. The quiet moments of obedience and diligence add weight to the record. The consistent refusal to compromise truth strengthens the testimony that a life presents. Eventually, that testimony begins to speak louder than any accusation.

Those who have observed closely recognize the pattern. They see the difference between a momentary claim and the long record of a person's character. What once seemed uncertain becomes clearer as the years reveal the consistency of the life being lived. In this way, a life answers questions long before a defense is ever required. The believer who understands this principle approaches life differently. Instead of focusing only on defending reputation in the moment, he focuses on living in a way that continually strengthens the record of his life.

Integrity becomes a daily choice.

Truth becomes a guiding principle.

Faithfulness becomes the path that shapes every decision. Over time, these choices form the testimony that will eventually stand before God.

This does not mean that a believer lives without struggle. Scripture is honest about the reality of weakness and the need for Grace. No life is free from moments that require repentance and restoration. We all have sinned and fallen short, so even repentance becomes part of the testimony.

A life that turns back to God when it stumbles demonstrates humility and trust. Grace becomes woven into the story of that life, showing not only human effort but divine transformation.

The testimony of such a life becomes powerful because it reflects both truth and redemption.

When the books are opened, the story that appears is not a single moment frozen in time. It is the full narrative of a life that has unfolded before God. The acts of faithfulness, the seasons of growth, and the moments of repentance. The perseverance that continued even when circumstances were difficult, all of these become part of the record.

For this reason, the Believer does not need to invent a defense when the time comes to give account. The testimony already exists. The life itself has been answering the questions all along.

Each day has added another line to the story. Each decision has strengthened the witness. Each act of faithfulness has contributed to the record that will stand before God. This is why the Scriptures encourage Believers to live with integrity in every circumstance. They are encouraged to begin and live with the desired end result in mind. The choices made today will one day appear as part of the testimony of a life.

When that testimony is examined, the truth will not depend on clever arguments or persuasive words. It will depend on what the life itself reveals. Because in the Court of God, a man does not stand with a defense prepared in a moment. He stands with the testimony of the life he has lived. His life has already pleaded his case.

PLEADING YOUR CASE BEFORE GOD

The phrase "plead your case" can sound unusual when applied to our relationship with God.

Many people imagine prayer as something very different—requests spoken in hope, petitions offered in need, or praise expressed in gratitude. All of these are important parts of prayer. Yet the Scriptures also reveal another dimension: moments when a person brings the circumstances of life before God and asks Him to examine them.

This is the language of a case.

The prophet Isaiah records God's invitation:

> Put Me in remembrance;
> let us contend together;
> state your case, that you may be acquitted.
> (Isaiah 43:26)

At first glance, this invitation may seem surprising. Why would the Creator of the universe invite human beings to present their case before Him?

The answer lies in the nature of God's Justice. God does not ask people to pretend that life is simple or that difficult situations do not exist. The Scriptures are filled with examples of men and women who spoke openly to God about the realities they faced. They brought their confusion, their suffering, their questions, and their hopes into His presence.

They did not hide the truth of their circumstances; they presented it. David often prayed in this way. Many of the Psalms read like the heartfelt testimony of a man describing the situation of his life before the Judge who sees all things. David spoke of enemies who misunderstood him, accusations that wounded him, and struggles that tested his faith.

Yet through all of these moments, David returned again and again to the same conviction: God knew the truth. Because God knew the truth, David could place the matter before Him and trust that justice ultimately belonged to the Lord. This is what it means to plead a case before God.

It does not mean arguing with God or attempting to persuade Him with clever reasoning. Instead, it means bringing the truth of one's life honestly into His presence. A person speaks openly about what has happened. They acknowledge their own failures when necessary. They describe the circumstances that have unfolded. They ask God to examine the matter in the light of His perfect knowledge.

In doing so, they place their confidence not in their own ability to control the outcome, but in the character of the Judge who sees everything clearly. This kind of prayer requires humility. It requires a willingness to speak truthfully about both strengths and weaknesses. It also requires trust that God's judgment will be just, even when the outcome is not immediately visible.

The Psalms provide many examples of this posture. Again and again, David places his life before God and asks the Lord to examine his heart. He invites God to test his motives, to search his thoughts, and to reveal whether his path is aligned with truth.

This kind of prayer is not defensive; it is transparent.

David understood that the Court of God operates differently from the courts of men. Human courts depend on limited evidence and imperfect understanding. God, however, sees the full story. Nothing is hidden from Him.

Because of this, pleading a case before God is not an attempt to convince Him of something He does not know. It is an act of trust that places the matter in the hands of the One who already knows the truth.

For the Believer, this practice transforms the way we respond to difficult situations. Instead of carrying the burden of proving ourselves to everyone around us, we bring the matter before God. Instead of allowing accusations or misunderstandings to dominate our thoughts, we place those concerns before the Judge who sees the entire record.

In His presence we speak honestly. We acknowledge what is true. And then we entrust the outcome to Him. Over time, this posture produces peace. The Believer who learns to place their case before God no longer feels compelled to control every narrative or correct every misunderstanding immediately. The need to win every argument fades when the heart is anchored in the confidence that God already knows the truth.

This does not mean that justice always appears quickly. Scripture shows that there are often seasons of waiting. David waited many years before the promises spoken over his life came to fulfillment. Joseph endured long years before the truth of his character was recognized. Yet both men trusted that the record of their lives was known before God.

In the end, that record spoke.

This is the quiet power of pleading a case before God. It shifts the focus from defending oneself before every human voice to living faithfully before the One whose judgment ultimately matters.

When the Believer brings the truth of their life into the presence of God, they are not asking Him to ignore justice. They are trusting Him to administer it perfectly. And when the time comes for the truth to be revealed, it will not depend on the arguments of a moment. It will depend on the testimony of a life that has been lived before Him.

EVIDENCE THAT SPEAKS

"As for Me and My House"

In every case, evidence eventually appears. Witnesses may speak, records may be examined, and arguments may be presented, but in the end the court looks for something simple: proof. Evidence reveals what words alone cannot fully establish.

In the life of a Believer, that evidence is found in the decisions that shape the direction of a life. One of the clearest examples of this appears in the words spoken by Joshua near the end of his leadership over Israel.

After guiding the people into the land God had promised, Joshua gathered the nation and challenged them to consider the direction of their future. They would need to decide whom they would serve. Would they follow the *gods* that earlier generations had worshiped, or would they remain faithful to the Lord who had brought them through the wilderness?

Joshua then made a declaration that has echoed through generations:

Choose for yourselves this day whom you will serve…
But as for me and my house, we will serve the Lord.
(Joshua 24:15)

These words were more than a statement. They were evidence.Joshua was not merely describing an idea or expressing a hope. He was declaring a direction that had already shaped his life. For decades he had followed the Lord faithfully—from the days when he served alongside Moses, through the wilderness years, and into the leadership of the nation. His life had already demonstrated the choice he was describing.

The declaration simply made visible what the evidence had been showing all along. This is how evidence functions in the testimony of a life. Decisions made consistently over time become proof of what a person truly values.

Anyone can make a promise in a moment of inspiration. Words spoken in a single day may sound impressive, but they must be confirmed by the pattern of life that follows. Joshua's declaration carried authority because it reflected decades of faithfulness. His leadership, his obedience, and his trust in God had already established the direction of his life.

The words simply revealed the evidence. This principle applies to every Believer. The testimony of a life is not formed by one dramatic moment. It is built through the daily decisions that quietly shape the path a person walks. Each choice to follow truth strengthens the evidence. Each act of faithfulness adds weight to the record.

Over time, the direction of a life becomes unmistakable.

A person who consistently chooses integrity demonstrates what they serve. A family that consistently honors God reveals the foundation upon which their house is built. A believer who continues to walk faithfully through difficulty shows where their trust truly rests. This kind of evidence does not rely on explanation. It speaks for itself.

When people observe a life shaped by these decisions, they begin to recognize something genuine. The consistency of the choices made becomes proof of what the person believes. Words are no longer required to convince others; the pattern of the life has already answered the question.

Joshua understood this. His declaration was not an attempt to persuade others through argument. It was the natural expression of a life already committed to serving the Lord. Because of that, his words carried weight. They were supported by the evidence of his life.

In the same way, the believer who lives faithfully before God gradually builds a testimony that speaks without the need for constant defense. The choices made within the home, the workplace, and the quiet spaces of everyday life begin to reveal the truth of what the heart serves.

Over time, that evidence becomes clear to those who are watching. More importantly, it becomes part of the record that stands before God.

When the books are opened, the direction of a life will already be visible. The decisions made day by day will reveal the path that was chosen. For those who follow Christ, the goal is not merely to make a declaration once in a lifetime. It is to live in such a way that the declaration becomes visible in every season.

"As for me and my house" becomes more than a statement. It becomes evidence. Because in the Court of God, the strongest proof of what a person believes is not found in the words they speak in a moment. It is found in the life they consistently live.

THE ROLE OF PATIENCE

In every court there is a period of waiting. Evidence may be gathered quickly, but judgment is rarely immediate. Witnesses must be examined. Records must be reviewed. The truth of a matter often becomes clearer as time allows the full story to unfold.

In the life of faith, this waiting can be one of the most difficult parts of trusting God's Justice.

When accusations arise or misunderstandings spread, the natural desire is for immediate resolution. We want the truth to be recognized quickly. We want the narrative to be corrected without delay. We hope for the moment when everything becomes clear and the record is set straight. Yet Scripture shows that the path of truth often includes seasons of patience.

Joseph is one of the clearest examples. After being falsely accused in Egypt, he was placed in prison for a crime he had not committed. The truth of his character was already established before God, yet years passed before the evidence of his integrity became visible to those around him.

During that time, Joseph did not control the narrative surrounding his life. He could not rewrite the story others believed. All he could do was continue living faithfully where he was placed. And that is exactly what he did.

Even in prison, Joseph acted with integrity. He served faithfully in the responsibilities given to him. The consistency of his character became visible to those who watched him closely. Over time, the evidence of his life began to speak louder than the accusation that had placed him there.

Eventually the truth emerged.

The same pattern appears in the life of David. Though he had been anointed king, David spent many years fleeing from Saul's pursuit. During that season, accusations against him circulated throughout the kingdom. Saul portrayed David as a threat, and many believed the narrative they heard. Yet David refused to take matters into his own hands. On more than one occasion he had the opportunity to kill Saul and end the conflict quickly. But David understood something important: the record of his life mattered more than immediate victory. He chose patience.

By refusing to act in anger, David preserved the integrity of his testimony. Over time, the truth of his character became evident to those who observed him.

Even Jesus experienced a season in which the truth about His life was not immediately recognized. Though He lived with perfect integrity, He endured accusation, rejection, and ultimately the injustice of the Cross. The story did not end there. The Resurrection revealed what had been true all along. These examples remind us that patience is often part of the process through which truth becomes visible.

The court of public opinion moves quickly. Narratives form in a moment and spread through the voices of those who repeat them. But the court of God is not rushed by the urgency of human expectations.

God allows time for the record of a life to become clear. This does not mean that patience is easy. Waiting can test faith deeply, especially when a person feels misunderstood or misrepresented. The temptation to force a resolution can become strong. Patience protects something very important: the integrity of the testimony. When a person refuses to abandon truth in order to achieve immediate vindication, their life continues to build evidence. Each decision to remain faithful strengthens the record that will eventually be examined.

Over time, that record begins to reveal the truth. People who observe closely begin to see patterns that cannot easily be denied. The consistency of a life lived with integrity becomes visible. What once seemed uncertain gradually becomes clear. Believers must trust the timing of God's Justice.

God does not forget what has been done. He does not overlook the details that others may miss. The record of a life remains before Him, even when circumstances appear unresolved. For the believer, patience becomes an act of trust. It reflects confidence that the truth of a life will eventually be seen. It acknowledges that God's judgment is not hurried, but it is always accurate. When the time comes for the record to be examined, the testimony of a life lived faithfully will speak. In that moment, the waiting will have served its purpose. Because patience allowed the evidence to grow.

And having in a readiness to revenge all disobedience, when your obedience is fulfilled. (2 Corinthians 10:6)

WHEN THE RECORD IS ENOUGH

There comes a moment in many cases when something important happens. The arguments stop. The questions fade. The court no longer needs additional explanation. The record itself is enough.

This moment does not always arrive quickly. It often follows seasons of accusation, misunderstanding, and patient endurance. During those earlier stages, the temptation to defend oneself repeatedly can feel overwhelming. Each new accusation seems to demand a response. Each misunderstanding seems to require correction.

Over time something begins to change.

The evidence of a life lived with integrity starts to accumulate. What once required explanation gradually becomes visible through the pattern of a person's conduct. People who observe closely begin to recognize the consistency of the life being lived. Decisions made in private begin to confirm what words alone could never fully prove.

Eventually, the record begins to speak for itself.

When that moment arrives, the need for constant defense begins to fade. The believer no longer feels compelled to answer every accusation or correct every narrative immediately. Not because truth no longer matters, but because the truth has already been demonstrated through the life that has been lived.

The record is sufficient.

This principle appears repeatedly in Scripture. Joseph did not spend the remainder of his life defending himself against the accusation that had once placed him in prison. The record of his wisdom and integrity eventually spoke so clearly that he was entrusted with leadership over the land of Egypt.

David did not spend his reign arguing about the accusations Saul had spread during earlier years. The evidence of David's leadership and faithfulness became visible to the nation he governed.

Even the ministry of Jesus revealed this pattern. Though accusations were raised against Him during His life, the record of His works—His teachings, His miracles, His compassion, and ultimately His resurrection—provided testimony that could not be silenced.

In each of these examples, the truth did not depend on the loudness of a defense. It depended on the evidence of a life.

For Believers today, this truth offers a profound kind of freedom. It releases us from the exhausting burden of managing every narrative about our lives. We no longer feel the need to chase every rumor or correct every misunderstanding immediately.

Instead, we focus on something far more important. We continue to live faithfully. Integrity today strengthens the record tomorrow. Faithfulness today becomes evidence that will eventually be seen. Over time, the testimony of a life lived before God grows stronger than any accusation that may have been spoken against it.

This does not mean that misunderstandings never occur again. Human opinion will always be imperfect, and narratives will continue to shift. But the believer whose life is grounded in truth understands that the ultimate record is not written by human voices.

It is preserved before God. When that record is examined, the evidence will be clear. The decisions made in private. The faithfulness maintained during difficult seasons. The integrity demonstrated when compromise would have been easier. All of these become part of the testimony that stands before the Judge who sees everything. At that point, words are no longer necessary. The life itself answers the questions. The evidence is already present, and the record is enough.

THE DAY THE BOOKS ARE OPENED

The Scriptures speak of a day when the record of every life will be examined. It is described not as chaos or confusion, but as a moment of order.

The Court is seated. The Judge takes His place. And the record that has been written over the course of a lifetime is brought forward. Daniel saw this moment in a vision in Daniel 7:10. The imagery is deliberate. Thrones are set. The Judge is present. The books are opened.

This is the moment when the testimony of a life is examined in the light of Truth.

Throughout life, many voices may attempt to define a person's story. Narratives may shift. Accusations may rise and fall. Public opinion may form conclusions based on partial information or misunderstanding. On this day, none of those shifting voices determine the outcome; the record does.

The books contain the testimony of what has actually been lived. Every decision, every act of faithfulness, every moment of obedience becomes part of the story that is revealed. Nothing essential is missing. Nothing true is forgotten.

The book of Revelation describes the same moment in even clearer terms.

> And I saw the dead, small and great, standing before God, and books were opened… and the dead were judged according to their works, by the things which were written in the books. (Revelation 20:12)

In that moment, the truth of every life becomes visible. For some, the opening of the books reveals a story shaped by rebellion and rejection of God's truth. For others, it reveals a life that has walked in faith, marked by repentance, obedience, and trust in the Grace provided through Christ.

In every case, the judgment rests on the truth of what has been lived. This is why Scripture encourages Believers to live with eternity in view. Begin with the end in mind. Live, but live with the end in mind. What results do you want? The choices made today become part of the testimony that will one day be examined. The quiet decisions that seem small in the moment become lines in a record that will not fade with time.

Life is writing its testimony every day.

For those who belong to Christ, the opening of the books does not bring fear in the way many people imagine. The believer's story is not merely a record of human effort; it is a record of Redemption in Christ Jesus.

Grace appears within the pages.

Moments of repentance reveal the work of transformation. Seasons of growth demonstrate the shaping hand of God within a life. Acts of faithfulness reflect the influence of the Spirit at work in the heart.

The story is not one of perfection. It is one of redemption. This is why the Believer can face that day with hope rather than dread. The testimony of their life is not examined apart from the work of Christ. The Advocate who intercedes on their behalf stands within the same court where the record is opened.

Justice and Mercy meet in that moment. The truth of a life is revealed, and the Grace that has shaped that life is also present. For this reason, the opening of the books is not merely a moment of judgment. It is also a moment of revelation. The truth that may have been questioned during life becomes unmistakably clear. The faithfulness that others overlooked becomes visible. The quiet integrity that went unnoticed is recognized before the Throne of God.

Every life tells a story. And on that day, the full story will be seen. The witnesses will have spoken. The record will have been preserved. The testimony will stand. Because when the books are opened, nothing about a life remains hidden. The truth will speak.

LIVING WITH THE RECORD IN MIND

When a person understands that **life** itself becomes testimony, something begins to change in the way they live. The awareness that every decision contributes to a larger record brings clarity to everyday choices. Situations that once seemed small or insignificant begin to take on deeper meaning. Words spoken in passing, actions taken in private, and responses formed in difficult moments all become part of the story that a life is telling.

Living with this awareness does not produce fear. Instead, it produces intentionality. A Believer who understands the reality of the record begins to approach life with a sense of purpose. Decisions are no longer guided merely by convenience or momentary emotion. They are shaped by the understanding that every choice contributes to the testimony of a life lived before God.

Integrity becomes a daily commitment rather than an occasional ideal. Truth becomes a foundation rather than a strategy. Faithfulness becomes the path that guides a person through both calm seasons and difficult ones.

This awareness also brings freedom from the pressure to impress others. When the primary concern is the record before God, the shifting opinions of people lose their power to control the direction of a life. The Believer no longer needs to chase approval or fear criticism. Public opinion rises and falls, but the testimony that matters most is the one written before the Throne of God.

This perspective changes the way a person responds to both praise and accusation. Praise no longer becomes a source of pride, and accusation no longer becomes a source of despair. Both are temporary voices in a world where narratives change quickly.

The record, however, remains steady. Living with the record in mind also shapes the environment of a home. The choices made within a family, the values practiced daily, and the example set before children and loved ones become part of a legacy that extends beyond a single lifetime.

Joshua understood this when he declared, "As for me and my house, we will serve the Lord." His words were not simply a declaration for that moment; they were a commitment that shaped the direction of his household. In the same way, every believer has the opportunity to shape the testimony of their life through the daily choices they make. Faithfulness practiced consistently becomes a witness that speaks long after individual moments have passed. Over time, the record grows, revealing a life that has been lived with Eternity in view.

THE CONFIDENCE OF A CLEAR TESTIMONY

There is a quiet confidence that comes from living with integrity.

It is not the loud confidence that seeks to prove itself to others, nor the fragile confidence that depends on constant approval. Instead, it is the steady assurance that grows from knowing that the life being lived is aligned with truth.

A person who lives this way does not need to construct elaborate defenses when questions arise. The testimony of their life already exists. The record has been forming through years of decisions that reflect integrity and faithfulness.

This confidence allows a believer to remain calm in situations where others might become defensive. When accusations appear, there is no immediate panic. When misunderstandings occur, there is no desperate attempt to control every conversation.

The life itself becomes the response. This does not mean that believers never experience difficulty or criticism. Scripture is clear that those who pursue truth will sometimes face opposition. Even the most faithful servants of God experienced seasons in which their character was questioned or their motives were misunderstood.

Yet those who continued walking in truth eventually discovered something powerful. The consistency of their lives spoke louder than the accusations that had once surrounded them.

Over time, people who observed closely began to recognize what was genuine. The patterns of faithfulness became visible. The integrity that had been practiced in private became evident in public. This is the quiet power of a clear testimony. It does not rely on forceful argument or persuasive speech. Instead, it rests on the accumulated evidence of a life that has consistently chosen truth.

For the Believer, this confidence also rests in the knowledge that God sees what others may overlook. The acts of faithfulness that pass unnoticed by the world remain fully visible before Him.

When the record of a life is examined, nothing that truly matters will be missing. Because of this, the believer can move forward without fear. The testimony of a life lived in truth provides a foundation that no accusation can permanently shake.

THE CASE IS COMPLETE

Every case eventually reaches its conclusion. The evidence has been presented. The witnesses have spoken. The record has been examined. At that point, the matter is ready to be decided.

In the Court of God, the conclusion of a life's story does not depend on the strength of a final argument. It rests on the testimony that has been formed over time. The record that appears before the Judge contains the story of what has actually been lived.

Each decision has contributed to that story. Each act of faithfulness has strengthened the testimony. Each moment of repentance has revealed the work of Grace within the heart. The life itself becomes the evidence.

For those who belong to Christ, this conclusion is not a moment of fear but a moment of fulfillment. The story of Redemption that has unfolded throughout their lives is fully revealed. The grace that shaped their journey becomes part of the testimony that stands before God.

The Advocate who has walked with them throughout their lives stands present in the same court where the record is examined.

Justice and Mercy meet.

Truth is revealed.

The story of a life becomes clear.

In that moment, the questions that once seemed complicated find their answer in the simple reality of what has been lived. The patterns of faithfulness, the seasons of growth, and the perseverance through difficulty all speak together as witnesses.

The case is complete. The testimony has been given. The life itself has told the story. Because in the end, a man does not stand before God with a defense prepared in a moment. He stands with the testimony of the life he has lived. That testimony speaks for him, pleading his case.

EPILOGUE

The Record That Remains

Long after words fade, a life continues to speak.

The conversations of a moment eventually disappear into memory. The arguments that once seemed urgent lose their intensity as time moves forward. Narratives that once shaped public opinion gradually give way to new stories and new voices.

But the testimony of a life remains. It remains in the choices that were made when no one was watching. It remains in the integrity that guided decisions when compromise would have been easier. It remains in the quiet faithfulness that continued through seasons of uncertainty and misunderstanding.

These moments become the lines of a story that cannot be erased. Scripture reminds us that God sees every part of that story. Nothing that is lived before Him is lost. The tears, the prayers, the sacrifices, and the acts of obedience that seemed small in the moment are all remembered.

They become part of a record that endures beyond the changing opinions of the world. For those who belong to Christ, that record tells a story of redemption. Grace appears within its pages. Moments of repentance reveal the transforming work of God. Seasons of faithfulness demonstrate the quiet strength that comes from trusting Him.

When the story of such a life is finally seen in its fullness, the truth will be unmistakable. A life lived before God has already given its testimony; and that testimony will remain.

Nothing is covered, that shall not be revealed; neither hid, that shall not be known. (Luke 12:2)

A man's life is his testimony. Let my life speak for me. And my living will not be in vain because I worked while it was day, for when the night comes, no man can work.

Your life is the witness.

Dear Reader

Thank you for acquiring and reading this book, I pray it has blessed you to even more begin and live with the desired outcome in mind. But live, to the Glory of God. **Continue the Journey.** This study guide accompanies the book: **Plead Your Case: A Man's Life Is His Testimony.** For deeper exploration of the biblical themes of witnesses, testimony, and the record of a life before God, readers are encouraged to read the full book.

Shalom,

Dr. Marlene Miles

Also recommended: THRONES: Not A Game

If you enjoyed this book, here are some new releases

Christ of God (*The*) 3-book series

Christ of God, (*The*) Box Set, includes all 3books

Other books on Authority:

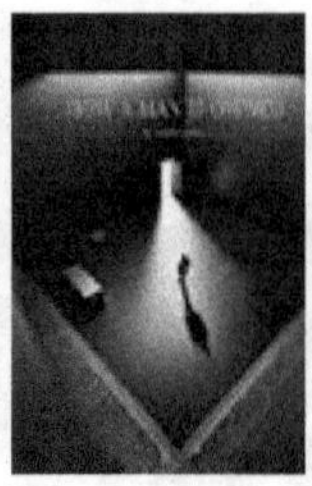

Prayerbooks by this author

There are some books that are only prayers. You just open up the book and pray.

Prayers Against Barrenness: *For Success in Business and Life*

Fruit of the Womb: *Prayers Against Barrenness*

Beauty Curses, *Warfare Prayers Against*
https://a.co/d/5Xlc20M

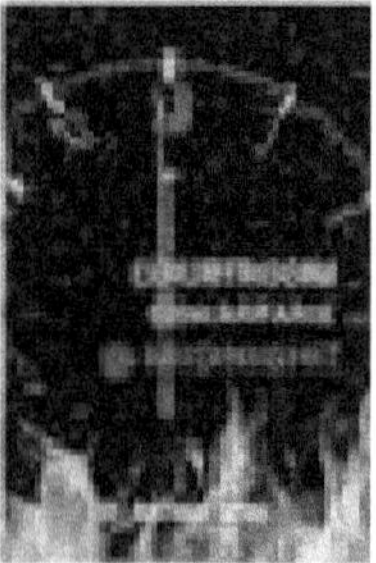

Courts of Marriage: Prayers for Marriage in the Courts of Heaven *(prayerbook)* https://a.co/d/cNAdgAq

Courtroom Warfare @ Midnight *(prayerbook)* https://a.co/d/5fc7Qdp

Demonic Cobwebs *(prayerbook)* https://a.co/d/fp9Oa2H

Every Evil Bird https://a.co/d/hF1kh1O

Gates of Thanksgiving

Spirits of Death, Hell & the Grave, Pass Over Me and My House

Throne of Grace: Courtroom Prayer

Warfare Prayer Against Poverty https://a.co/d/bZ61lYu

Prayer Manuals

FAKE FRIENDS: *Prayers Against Betrayers*

HOLIDAY WARFARE Prayer Manual (humorous) Surviving Family Gatherings All Year Long (without catching a case)

SOUL TIE Prayer Manual (The) Part of a 3-part series including a workbook.

MAD at DADDY Prayer Manual – part of a 3-part series including a workbook.

Healing the Sibling & Relative Wound Prayer Manual

Healing the Father-Son Wound Prayer Manual

Breaking Curses of the Mother Prayer Manual

Other books by this author

Abundance of Jesus (The) https://a.co/d/5gHJVed

AK: The Adventures of the Agape Kid

Already Married in the Spirit: *Why You May Not Be Married in the Natural*

AMONG SOME THIEVES https://a.co/d/dkYT4ZV

Ancestral Powers

Anti-Marriage, *The Spirit of*

Backstabbers https://a.co/d/gi8iBxf

Barrenness, *Prayers Against* https://a.co/d/feUltIs

Battlefield of Marriage, *The*

Beware of the Dog: Prayers Against Dogs in the Dream.

Bless Your Food: *Let the Dining Table be Undefiled* *https://a.co/d/6oPMRDv*

Blindsided: *Has the Old Man Bewitched You?* https://a.co/d/5O2fLLR

Break Free from Collective Captivity

Broken Spirits & Dry Bones

By Means of a Whorish Father

Caged Life: Get Out Alive! https://a.co/d/bwPbksX

Casting Down Imaginations

Christ of God (*The*) 3-book series

Christ of God, (*The*) Box Set, includes all three books

Churchzilla, The Wanna-Be, Supposed-to-be Bride of Christ https://a.co/d/eAf5j3x

Collateral Damage: ***When What Happened Spiritually Was Your Fault***

Demonic Cobwebs (prayerbook)

Demonic Time Bombs

Demons Hate Questions

Devil Loves Trauma, *The*

Devil Weapons: Unforgiveness, Bitterness,…

The Devourers: Thieves of Darkness 2

Do Not Swear by the Moon

Don't Refuse Me, Lord (4 book series)

https://a.co/d/idP34LG

Dream Defilement

The Emptiers: *Thieves of Darkness, 1*
https://a.co/d/5I4n5mc

Entanglements: Illegal Knots Limiting Your Life

Evil Touch

Failed Assignment

Fantasy Spirit Spouse https://a.co/d/hW7oYbX

FAT Demons (The): *Breaking Demonic Curses*
https://a.co/d/4kP8wV1

The Fold (5-book series)

- The Fold (Book 1)
- Name Your Seed (Book 2)
- The Poor Attitudes of Money (3)
- Do Not Orphan Your Seed (4)
- For the Sake of the Gospel (5)
- My Sowing Journal

Gang Ups: Touch Not God's Anointed

Gathered: No Longer Scattered
https://a.co/d/1i5DPIX

Getting Rid of Evil Spiritual Food

https://a.co/d/i2L3WYQ

got HEALING? Verses for Life

got LOVE? Verses for Life https://a.co/d/8seXHPd

got HOPE? Verses for Life

got money? https://a.co/d/g2av41N

Has My Soul Been Sold? https://a.co/d/dyB8hhA

Here Come the Horns: *Skilled to Destroy* https://a.co/d/cZiNnkP

Hidden Sins: Hidden Iniquity

https://a.co/d/4MthOwa

How to Dental Assist

How to Dental Assist2: Be Productive, Not Wasteful

How To Stay Prayed Up

How to STOP Being a Blind Witch or Warlock

I Take It Back

In Multiplying I Will Multiply Thee

Into Freedom:

Irresistible: Jesus' Triumphal Entry
https://a.co/d/d09IfEC

KNOW YOUR BATTLE: Stop Swinging Blindly — and Win Against Opponents, Adversaries & Enemies (Workbook) https://a.co/d/eOwFKlV

Legacy

Let Me Have A Dollar's Worth https://a.co/d/h8F8XgE

Level the Playing Field

Living for the NOW of God https://a.co/d/6bK5duE

Lose My Location https://a.co/d/crD6mV9

Love Breaks Your Heart

Mad At Daddy: Healing Father-Wounds that Affect Motherhood (book, workbook & prayer manual)

Made Perfect In Love

Mammon https://a.co/d/29yhMG7

Man Safari, *The*

Marriage Ed.: *Rules of Engagement & Marriage*

Made Perfect in Love

Money Hunters: Beware of Those

Money on the Altar https://a.co/d/4EqJ2Nr

Mulberry Tree, *The* https://a.co/d/9nR9rRb

Motherboard (The) - *Soul Prosperity Series*

Name Your Seed

Occupy: *Until I Return* https://a.co/d/bZ7ztUy

One Defining Day*: A Day When Dreams Come True*

Opponent, Adversary, or Enemy?: Fight The Right Battle with the Right Weapons

https://a.co/d/byQqEE2 & companion workbook: Know Your Battle

Plantation Souls

Players Gonna Play

Portals: Shut the Front Door: Prayers to Close Evil Portals.

Power Money: Nine Times the Tithe

https://a.co/d/gRt41gy

The Power to Get Wealth https://a.co/d/e4ub4Ov

Powers Above

The Robe, Part 1, The Lessons of Joseph

The Robe, Part II, The Lessons of Joseph

Seasons of Grief

Seasons of Siege: God Is Coming

Seasons of Waiting

Seasons of War

Second Marriage, Third--, *Any Marriage*

https://a.co/d/6m6GN4N

Seducing Spirits: Idolatry & Whoredoms

https://a.co/d/4Jq4WEs

Shut the Front Door: *Prayers to Close Portals*
https://a.co/d/cH4TWJj

Siege: *God Is Coming*

Sift You Like Wheat

The Silences of God:

Six Men Short: What Has Happened to all the Men?

SLAVE

Sleep Afflictions & Really Bad Dreams https://a.co/d/f8sDmgv

Soul Prosperity soul prosperity series 3

https://a.co/d/5p8YvCN

Soul Ties: How Soul Ties Form, and How To Break Them (book, workbook & prayer manual)

Souls In Captivity

The Spirit of Anti-Marriage

The Spirit of Poverty https://a.co/d/abV2o2e

Spiritual Thieves https://a.co/d/eqPPz33

StarStruck- Triangular Power series.

SUNBLOCK- Triangular Power series.

The Swallowers: *Thieves of Darkness*, 3

Take It Back

This Is NOT That: How to Keep Demons from Coming at You

Time Is of the Essence

Too Many Wives: *Why You Have Lady Problems*

Tormenting Spirits https://a.co/d/dAogEJf

Toxic Souls

Triangular Power *(series),* Powers Above, SUNBLOCK, Do Not Swear by the Moon, STARSTRUCK

TRIBE: *What Covenants Are Governing You…?*

Unbreak My Heart: *Don't Let Me Die*

Uncontested Doom

Ungovered Hunger: How Unchecked Appetite Dismantles Authority

Unguarded Hours, *The*

Unseen Life, *The* (forthcoming)

Upgrade: How to Get Out of Survival Mode Toxic Souls (Book 2 of series) , Legacy (Book 3 of series)

The Wasters: *Thieves of Darkness,* Bk 2
https://a.co/d/bUvI9Jo

What Have You to Declare? What Do You Have With You from Where You've Been?

When I Was A Child, *I Prayed As a Child*

When the Devourer is Rebuked
https://a.co/d/1HVv8oq

When The Table Is Set Against You

WTH? Get Me Out of This Hell
https://a.co/d/a7WBGJh

The Wilderness Romance *(series)* This series is about conducting a Godly relationship and marriage with someone who is a Wilderness person. ***The Social Wilderness***

- ***The Sexual Wilderness***
- ***The Spiritual Wilderness***

Other Series

The Fold (a series on Godly finances) https://a.co/d/4hz3unj

Soul Prosperity Series https://a.co/d/bz2M42q

Spirit Spouse **books**

https://a.co/d/9VehDSo

https://a.co/d/97sKOwm

Battlefield of Marriage, The

https://a.co/d/eUDzizO

Players Gonna Play

https://a.co/d/2hzGw3N

Sent Spirit Spouse (can someone send you a spirit spouse? This book is not yet released.)

Matters of the Heart, Made Perfect in Love https://a.co/d/70MQW3O , Love Breaks Your Heart https://a.co/d/4KvuQLZ, Unbreak My Heart https://a.co/d/84ceZ6M Broken Spirits & Dry Bones https://a.co/d/e6iedNP

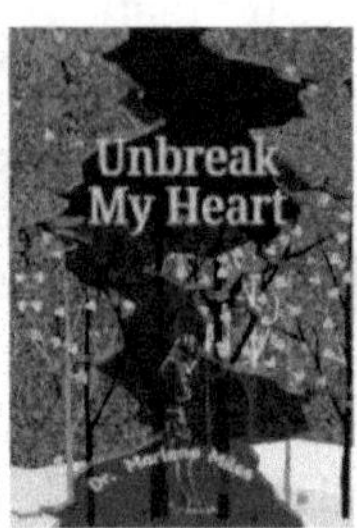

Thieves of Darkness series

The Emptiers https://a.co/d/heioOdO

The Wasters https://a.co/d/5TG1iNQ

The Swallowers https://a.co/d/1jWhM6G

The Devourers: Why We Can't Have Nice Things https://a.co/d/87Tejbf

Spiritual Thieves

Red Flags: The Track Is Not Safe (book & workbook)

Triangular Powers https://a.co/d/aUCjAWC

Upgrade (series) *How to Get Out of Survival Mode* https://a.co/d/aTERhX0

We Get Along, Right? Compatibility for Couples – (book & workbook)

Dr. Marlene Miles is a teacher, author, and spiritual thinker known for her grounded, discerning approach to prayer and spiritual formation. Her work emphasizes clarity, restraint, and maturity in faith—helping believers move beyond emotionalism and performance into a steady, practiced walk with God.

With a deep respect for Scripture and a practical understanding of daily life, Dr. Miles writes for those who want their prayer life to be formed, not dramatized. Her teaching encourages spiritual maintenance, discernment, and responsibility—so faith remains strong not only in crisis, but in everyday living.

www.ingramcontent.com/pod-product-compliance
Lightning Source LLC
LaVergne TN
LVHW010948110826
845149LV00015B/3254

* 9 7 8 1 9 7 1 9 3 3 4 4 3 *